James D. Elderkin

Biographical Sketches and Anecdotes of a Soldier of three Wars

James D. Elderkin

Biographical Sketches and Anecdotes of a Soldier of three Wars

ISBN/EAN: 9783337307264

Printed in Europe, USA, Canada, Australia, Japan

Cover: Foto ©Thomas Meinert / pixelio.de

More available books at **www.hansebooks.com**

BIOGRAPHICAL SKETCHES

AND

ANECDOTES

OF

A SOLDIER OF THREE WARS,

AS WRITTEN BY HIMSELF.

———————

THE FLORIDA, THE MEXICAN WAR AND THE GREAT
REBELLION, TOGETHER WITH SKETCHES OF
TRAVEL, ALSO OF SERVICE IN A MILI-
TIA COMPANY AND A MEMBER
OF THE DETROIT LIGHT
GUARD BAND FOR
OVER THIRTY
YEARS.

——— — ——

BY

JAMES D. ELDERKIN.

DETROIT, MICH.

MAY 1, 1899.

Biographical Sketches and Anecdotes,

BY

MAJOR J. D. ELDERKIN,

A VETERAN OF THREE WARS.

———

MY BIRTH PLACE AND BOYHOOD DAYS.

I was born near Salmon River, N. Y., December 16, 1820, and was brought up at Baldwinsville, town of Lysander, Onondaga Co., N. Y. My father was a carpenter and joiner, and a sound Jackson Democrat. He lived to seventy years of age, and could have run a footrace the day before his death. He was of Scotch lineage, and the sturdy Scotchman could be seen in his every move. Up to my fourteenth year I remained at home helping my father and attending school some; but being of a restless nature, I left home at fourteen years of age, or in 1834. I remained away about a year. During this year of absence I spent most of the time as a driver on the Erie canal.

A STARTLING EXPERIENCE.

My first experience was a startling and dangerous one: A man from Baldwinsville, whom I knew well, and who was part owner of a boat, employed me as a driver. The captains name was Tarbox. We were carrying lumber from Fulton to Albany. The first morning I started out nearly put an end to my career as a canal driver, and also of my life. We had loaded the boat while in the Oswego river, and were about to enter the canal. When the captain told me he would take charge of my team and I should go on the boat and cast off the towline. This was in consequence of our entering a lock, which would take us from the river into the canal. The team I was driving was a young and spirited team. I went to the bow of the boat to execute the order and stood with my back to the cabin, ignorant of what might take place. The team gave a sudden jerk and detached the plank I was leaning against and I was hurled into the river. The boat hit me on the head and back and doubled me up. The depth of water saved my life. Had it been in the canal, it would have killed me. At any rate, it was a narrow escape, as I could not swim a stroke, but soon struck bottom and fished myself out by wading ashore.

After we unloaded at Albany and started on our return trip we went very slow, only using one horse and not running nights. The forward cabin was used for the horses and the after cabin for a dining-room and sleeping room. For a long distance the canal runs parallel with the Mohawk river, and is very high, sometimes fifty feet above the river. On this occasion, as we were passing through Little Falls, we were just coming out of a lock, when the towline broke and the horse went down the embankment. It killed the horse and nearly killed me. I felt the effects of the fall for years after.

The above represent a few of my many narrow escapes; and no wonder, for Prof. Lyman E. Stowe, the astrologer, and an old comrade, tells me I was born in the sign "Sagittarius," the sign of accidents, and that I was destined to experience many narrow escapes from accidents. Whether or not there is any truth in astrology I do not know, but certain it is that I have met with a great number of narrow escapes from serious injury and death from accidents.

After a year of tough experience for a boy I returned to Baldwinsville; but upon returning I found no home, my mother having died before my first departure, my father's family was scattered, and I found no place to go when I returned, so I immediately went to my brother John's house. My brother John was an architect and builder—just starting out in business life.

One morning I went over where he was working, and finding him laying out timber, I thought I might make myself useful, and so picked up a corner chisel and began mortising timber. My brother came over and called my attention to the nature of the timber, and cautioned me, saying: "Be very careful or you may break the chisel." I replied: "All right; but I think there is no danger." But, alas! a moment after the chisel snapped. I was so dumbfounded I knew not what to do. Such a chisel, in those days, cost several dollars, and I had no money to purchase a new one for him, and I could not face him with the misfortune, and so fled. I did not see him again for thirteen years, until I returned from the Mexican war. He then came to Detroit to see me, and almost the first words he said, as he shook hands, was: "The last time I saw you, I just got a glimpse of your coat tail as you flitted around the corner." And he laughed at me heartily.

After the incident of the chisel I thought I had no place on earth where I was welcome. I now started out on a life of wandering, which lasted for many years. Having no money, I was compelled to take a little of the experience of a tramp. My first employment was on the Erie canal, near Schenectady, N. Y., as a driver of a horse and cart. I stopped here for a short time and again commenced my wanderings for a better position. I got employment for a time in a livery stable, and afterwards, for a time, at the Mansion House, Utica, N. Y.; but I soon started on again. Having but very little money, I soon ran out of funds, and my experience as a tramp began to be severe indeed, until one day, while wandering in the streets of Schenectady a kindly old gentleman asked me if I would like a bowl of clam soup, as I was standing outside smelling the soup. I replied that I would, and I think I never eat anything I thought tasted quite as good. While in the restaurant a couple of United States soldiers came in. I asked them if they knew of any one that wanted a boy for work, and they in turn asked me how I would like to become a soldier. I replied that I would like it. I thought anything would be preferable to the life of a tramp I was living.

I was nineteen years of age, for this was in 1839; but the officer told me I would have to claim I was twenty-one years old or I could not enlist. This, of course, I did, and a few days later became one of Uncle Sam's soldiers.

When quite a lad, I liked to play the flute, and one of the pleasant memories of my boyhood days was of sitting on the banks of the Seneca river, with my feet in the water, and while playing the flute the fish would nibble at my toes and perform other amusing antics while seemingly attracted by the music of my flute. And while my calls on the fish were quite regular, if I chanced to be late I would find them actually jumping out of the water, as if to see if I were coming.

This practice with the flute turned out to be of great service to me while in the army, as my music was always in demand.

We remained at the recruiting office with Lieut. Prince, the recruiting officer, for about two months, and then went to Bedloes Island, where we remained for two or three days.

The only incident of note to me that transpired here was the loss of my last suit of underwear, which I washed and hung on the line, keeping my eyes on them while they dried. But, alas! I went to dinner, to return and find my underwear gone. This loss was nearly irreparable for a time, as I could not draw on the government to replace them until we arrived at some regular barracks. But through the kindness of Sergt. Head, who gave me a suit of his own, I was saved from the winter blasts that howled through the rigging of the ship St. Mary, which we now boarded to be taken to New Orleans.

We were two weeks making our trip from New York to New Orleans. For the most of the way the weather was very bad; it was so bad that the cooks could not get us a warm meal, and we lived on hard-tack and raw pork. But at last it cleared up and we were bowling along in the Gulf of Mexico under a spanking breeze and a magnificent setting sun, when I noticed a little black speck of a cloud arising above the horizon not large enough to make a man a shirt, as the sailors say; but in less than five minutes the sky was overcast and a blizzard struck our good ship and threw her on her beam's end and the sails partially under water, when I heard the captain's cry, as he came from the cabin: "Let go the halyard." The good ship righted, but her ballast was so shifted that she rode the rest of the way into port nearly on her side, showing her bottom to the sun. Of course none of us ever expected to reach port, but we were saved, or I could not narrate this incident here.

We remained at New Orleans but two days, when we took a steamer down the Mississippi river to the mouth of the Arkansas river, thence up past Little Rock to the Grand river and to Fort Gibson, which was then in the wilds of Arkansas and Indian Territory, and was in the Cherokee nation. Here I joined my regiment, the Fourth United States Infantry, Company D, and this regiment was my home for fifteen years. The regiment was under the command of Maj. Stanford. We remained at this post two years.

Perhaps a few incidents of our camp life there will interest the reader:

Lieut. ———— was the adjutant of our regiment; a very fine appearing man, but not well liked by the men, and we will let the reader judge of his merits by one of his dastardly acts.

The Grand river rises away up in the Rocky Mountains, and is a stream of beautiful, clear, cold water. On the west side of the river the Creek nation was stationed, and on the east side the Cherokee nation. These Indians were well mixed with the whites, and consequently well civilized. Just above the fort the river was crossed by a ferry. A hawser was stretched across the river and a large flat boat used for the ferry. This was attached to the hawser by ropes and pulleys. By drawing the bow of the boat well up stream the swift current propelled the boat across.

The charges for crossing the river, to white men, was one dollar. The Indians could cross free. I was detailed as corporal of the squad that had the boat in charge, and hence was in position to take particular note of the incident I am about to relate.

The chief of the Creek nation was the father of the noblest and most beautiful maiden I ever saw. She was half white and every inch a lady. Adjt. —— fell in love with and married her, and lived with her two years, and it was then currently reported that he cruelly abandoned her; but he paid the penalty with his life, as he was shot through the heart at the battle of Monterey, Mex.

Many a time I have watched that fine pair ride over the lovely prairies on a wolf hunt. I have watched the beautiful plumes in her hat waving in the sunlight as far as the eye could reach.

She often crossed the river from the fort to see her father, when she would invariably call me to her and say: "Now, corporal, here is a dollar for my fare. Put it in your pocket. Do not give it to the adjutant, as I am an Indian and have a right to go free; so you keep the dollar for yourself." The perfect ladyship of this beautiful woman was remarked by the whole regiment, and their indignation was expressed at her cruel abandonment.

While stationed at Fort Gibson we built the military road to Fort Smith, ninety miles below us. To protect the men from malaria, the government served a gill of whisky daily to each man; but, of course, there were men in the regiment who hankered for more, and could never be satisfied until they could drink no more. So on pay days they would soon be found intoxicated if they could possibly get the whisky to get drunk on. On one occasion, just after pay day, Capt. Buchanan, of Company B, an officer everybody liked, was officer of the day.

Corporal Stokes, of Company B, reported with his detail for duty. Capt. Buchanan inquired: "Who have you in your detail?" the corporal replied: "I have Jack Harron." "Look out for him," said the captain. "Tom Crask," continued the corporal. "Look out for him," said the captain. "Jimmy Bar," again said the corporal. "Look out for him," repeated the captain. "James McDonough," concluded the corporal. "Oh, Oh!" exclaimed the captain with a long low whistle; and turning to his lieutenant said, "Mr. Hammond, the camp will be taken to-night sure."

Now, these were all intelligent men, literary men, actors, and that class of men who had drifted into the army, and they were the life of the regiment. But their weakness was their love of the ardent.

In the night, when the captain made his rounds, he found Jack Harron walking his beat, but he was as drunk as a lord and looking as wild as an Indian, for he had a red handkerchief tied around his head. "Who goes there?" challenged Harron. "Officer of the day," came the reply. "Advance, officer of the day, and give the countersign." This was done. Then the officer of the day asked: "Mr. Harron, where is your beat?" "Let the captain stand out of the way and I'll show him," was the reply, as Jack staggered over his beat. "Where are the rest of the men?" inquired the captain. "There lies Corp. Stokes," said Harron, "and the rest are lying around here sleeping." "But I can't find any of them," said the captain. And Corp. Stokes was so drunk that he could get nothing but a grunt out of him.

The next day the captain ordered the grog stopped for all of these men as a punishment. When rations were served and no grog for these men, McDonald took it to heart very hard and inquired why it was stopped. The sergeant told him the captain ordered it as a punishment on account of their absence from duty. McDonald immediately called on the captain and said: "Captain, the sergeant tells me you ordered my grog stopped." "Yes," replied the captain, "I stopped it on account of your absence from duty last night." "But, captain," exclaimed McDonald with an air of grave injured innocence, "I can prove I was not absent, but was sleeping." "Who can you prove it by?" inquired the captain. "By Jimmy Bar," emphatically declared McDonald. "Oh! Can you prove it by someone else?" asked the captain. "Oh, yes; by Jack Harron," again replied McDonald. "Well,

you can have your grog. I had rather allow it to
you than seek for further proof," said the captain, for
he could see it was useless to try to prove anything
against these men, who were ready to swear for each
other through thick and thin. But the captain must
surely have thought he could not believe his senses,
and that it was he, and not the men, who were drunk.

PRIVATE RYAN AND GEN. TAYLOR.

Gen. Taylor, off duty, appeared like a very plain
citizen, and on one occasion, when he called on his
rounds of inspection, it was just after pay day, and
Jack Ryan, one of the jolly drinkers, went in search
of whisky. He met Gen. Taylor. Not knowing him,
he inquired of him where he could get some whisky.
"Well," said the general, "over yonder are the women's
quarters. I think if you go over there and inquire you
can get some." Away went Jack, and, sure enough,
he soon came back with his flask full; and approaching the general, said: "Here, old man, I got some.
For your kindness, take a drink with me." "No, no,"
replied the general. "Put it up quick, or some of the
officers may see you with it and take it away from you
and put you in the guardhouse."

The next day, while in line for inspection, Jack, of course, saw the general, and inquired: "Who is that man?" Several who knew replied: "Why, that is Old Tonkey" (Gen. Taylor). Tonkey was the soldiers' pet name for their loved old general. "Oh, my God!" said Jack. "I'm killed; I'm killed. That is the man I inquired of where to get the whisky, and he told me where to get it, too." But, of course, there was nothing more ever heard of the matter.

We were now ordered to Old Point Comfort, where we rested a short time before starting for Florida to engage in the Seminole war.

WHILE HERE A STARTLING ESCAPADE TOOK PLACE.

With one or two exceptions, the officers of the Fourth United States Infantry were well liked by the men as well as by the citizens. But we had one officer, Capt. L——, of Company I, who was a petty tyrant.

Capt. L—— was drilling his company one morning, and one man had been drinking a little too much, and it angered the captain, so he ordered him to stand in

front of his quarters at a shoulder arms. The man
stood there for a long time, until he got tired and
brought his gun down to an order. The captain, seeing him, immediately ordered him to come to a shoulder. But the man said, "I cannot, captain; I am exhausted." The captain intimated he was the son of a
female dog, and told him to bring his gun to his
shoulder or he would run him through with his
sword. The man did not obey quick enough to please
the captain, and he made a thrust with his sword; but
the man was too quick for him and stabbed the captain in the groin with his bayonet. Of course this
was insubordination, and must be punished. The
soldier knew this, and was determined to escape. A
chase and struggle ensued, but the man was captured
and bound; he soon was courtmartialed and sentenced
to be shot. The day for execution arrived, and twelve
men were detailed as the fireing party. The man was
led out and placed upon his coffin and the fireing
party ordered to fire. But they were in sympathy with
the man, and fired over his head. Immediately afterward a horseman came riding at full speed, shouting
that the man had been reprieved by the President. The
man was discharged and ordered to leave; but the

citizens were so indignant over the whole proceeding that they raised $500 and gave it to the man before he left.

This same Capt. L—— was suddenly taken sick just before our first engagement with the Seminoles. A year afterwards, when we were in California, he used to order a detail of men to row him around in the waters of Puget Sound, and on one occasion there came up a sudden squal and overturned the boat, and the whole party was drowned, and that was the end of Capt. L——, of Company I.

The Indian war, known as the "Seminole," or "Florida War," broke out in 1835, and lasted until 1842.

IN THE SEMINOLE WAR.

In 1841, the Fourth United States Infantry was ordered to Florida to take part in that war. From Fort Gibson we went to New Orleans. There we took a steamer, which landed us at Tampa Bay, where we remained about two months, and then took up our line of march in our first campaign in the Florida war.

I am inclined to think if our boys who were engaged

in the recent little affair with Spain could taste a bit
of our Florida experience they would think their recent war experience was quite a pleasant picnic in
comparison. Let it be remembered, at that early day,
Florida was, for the most part, a howling wilderness,
and indescribable in its wild yet horrible and beautiful
grandure. For the most part, it was a succession of
swamps, ridges, lagoons and low hills, called hummocks. The timber land, except for a trail here and
there, was an impenetrable jungle. Especially was
this the case in the swamps, where the mighty cypress
often from four to five feet in diameter, raised its giant
head high above the dense and tangled thorn-clad vine
and shrubbery beneath, as if its mighty foliage was not
enough to shut out the sunlight, each limb being hung
heavy with Spanish moss, shutting out every ray of
light, bringing the gloom of night over a trail beset
with thorns, rattlesnakes and deadly moccasins gliding
over your feet and ready to strike if trod upon.

Not only this, but every leaf seemed to bear some
poisonous insect as dangerous as the serpents under
foot, and still more dangerous than all the rest, the
cunning redskins had slowly retreated before the
United States army; for this war had been going on

for years, and they had penetrated the jungles deep, and here and there cleared the hummocks of timber and built themselves comfortable homes from the bark of the cypress tree; and they defended those homes with that fury that only men driven to desperation can do. Concealing themselves under the dense foliage, covered with Spanish moss, they were undiscernable until they revealed their position by a rifle shot. This, of course, was often too late for some poor comrade who was pushing his way determindly through the tangle, and with death lurking on every hand. Wherever there had chanced to be a clearing of some daring settler's once happy home, now nothing remained but blackened ruins, a standing chimney or, perchance, here and there an orange grove, laden with fruit, as it peeped above the tangled underbrush, seemingly arising to strangle every relic of civilized man.

The night was made hideous by the howl of wolves, the scream of the panther, the bull-like bellow of the alligator and the dismal cry of the loon, interspersed here and there by the sweet notes of the whippoorwill, or the song of the American nightingale, that most beautiful of all songsters, the mocking bird. (The mocking bird often sings in the night.)

All of these sounds, whether dismal or sweet, were heeded with the greatest precaution, as it might be real or might be the signal of a wily savage to his cohorts to join in an onslaught that would end in a massacre or death-struggle of extermination for one side or the other.

Wherever clearings were found, or the higher ground lessened the density of the foliage, the graceful magnolia spread her beautiful branches of velvet leaves and magnificent blossoms, which ladened the air with perfume so sweet and heavy that it could be scented miles away; and high among the branches carroled the sweetest songsters man ever heard as they flitted from limb to limb under the glorious sunlight overhead, as if to emphasize to man that a glowing picture of hell and heaven might exist on earth before his very eyes.

The above is a weak attempt to describe the awful grandeur of Florida in those terrible times of savage warfare.

It was in 1841 we went to Florida, where we remained for one year. Of all my experience of hardships in three wars that which I experienced in Florida was the worst.

We left Tampa Bay and took our line of march to the Everglades. We were accompanied by our wagons bearing provisions and camp equipage as far as it was possible for wagons to go, then they were left behind and pack mules substituted to carry the absolute necessities, which was chiefly powder and lead and some extra rations of hardtack and pork. We were soon compelled to abandon our mules and load ourselves down with ammunition and provisions. With this tremendous load of ammunition equipments and five days' rations of pork and hardtack, we wallowed through the brier and bush and mud and water day after day.

We, of course, had no tents, and when the storms appeared to be likely to be too heavy we cut down palm trees and used the branches to build shelter, while we used the cabbage-like top for food to stretch out our rations as far as possible, and only for that, I think, we should have starved. Though there was not much neutriment to it, it furnished the bulk, so we did not feel so gaunt. The palm was cut in small pieces and boiled as you would boil cabbage, though it did not require so much boiling as cabbage.

We had a number of Indian guides, who followed the trail of the Indians as unerringly as a hound would follow a deer. They were always in advance until they noticed the water ran roily, knowing thereby the retreating Indians were near, when the Indian scouts would drop to the rear and we were pushed to the front to give battle.

Our first engagement will forever remain as fresh in my memory as the day it occurred.

We were about to enter the fight when Capt. L——, of Company I, whom I have mentioned before, was suddenly taken sick. As he was not liked at all, the boys would have it that he showed the white feather. Eight men were detailed to take him back to the depot where we left the mules. This was done by constructing a stretcher by binding a blanket on two poles and leaving the ends of the poles projecting out for handles, two men carrying him some distance, when they would be relieved by two others, and so on. We were now fully fifty miles in the heart of the great cypress swamp. Sergt. Douain and ten men were detailed to take the advance. I chanced to be one of those men, Sergt. Douain taking the lead and I following. We had not advanced far when the sergeant was shot and killed. He was the first man killed in that campaign. He was a member of my company. We were marching in the water knee deep when we were fired upon. Though we lost several men, not an Indian could be seen. We pushed on to the dry land as fast as possible, but when we got there the Indians had concluded to retreat farther into the wilderness. We followed them some distance, and then returned to the island, where we buried our dead by carrying them out into deep water and driving stakes over them to keep the bodies down so in case the Indians did come back they could not find them and mutilate the bodies: We were continually marching through water knee deep and upward; and I must relate an amusing incident of

CORP. YOUNG AND MAJ. BELKNAP.

The officers of our regiment were generally pretty well liked, but Maj. Belknap, who had our expedition in charge, belonged to the Seventh United States Infantry, and just before we started on our expedition our rations of coffee were taken from us and rye coffee substituted. This did not please the men very well, and they declared Maj. Belknap had sold the coffee and furnished rye instead, pocketing the difference. Whether this was so or not, the men generally thought it was true, and every morning made the woods ring with their cries of "Rye coffee! Rye coffee!" It was very evident that the major thought no more of a private soldier than if he were a dog. and these morning salutations did not increase his amiable disposition toward them; but for all this Maj. Belknap was a brave, self-reliant fellow. Be it known there are always some men ready to sacrifice manhood to carry favor with those in power. Corp. Young, of Company D, was one of these fellows, and on one occasion when we were marching through water knee deep the corporal slid out of his place in the ranks and hastened forward and said: "Major, there is a deep hole just in front of you." For his pains the major turned and sharply asked: "What company do you belong to?" "Company D," replied the corporal. "Join your company immediately and never leave the ranks without orders," was the sharp command. The corporal came back to the ranks much crestfallen for the attention of the men had all been called to the episode. But a

moment afterward the corporal experienced some returning satisfaction by seeing the major plunge to the
armpits in the deep hole, sharply crying as he went
down: "Hip no bottom." But he laughingly pulled
himself out of the hole, and it was well that he could
do so, for he was so cordially hated that hardly a man
would have went to his assistance.

OUR RETURN.

We were now entirely out of rations and were compelled to return to the depot where we left the mules.
Thus ended our first campaign.

OUR SECOND CAMPAIGN.

We remained at this camp but a day and then
started on our second campaign. We went up to Cin-
able river by taking a steamboat at a point then called
Point "Arresser." Getting on or off from a boat was a
serious business, as there were no docks and the banks
were muddy. The men were taken off in small boats,
but horses and mules were thrown overboard and they
swam to shore. The place selected for a camp was in

CARRYING DESPATCHES TO GEN. WORTH, FORT KING.

a pine woods so dense with underbrush that we were compelled to dig trees up by the roots, which were five inches in diameter, before we could pitch our tents; and the rattlesnakes were so thick that we were compelled to keep on the watch continually to prevent being bitten.

We stocked the steamboat with wood, carrying it on our shoulders. After establishing a depot there, we again took up our line of march in pursuit of the Indians. This time we had a much larger force than before. We had about five hundred men, commanded by Col. Garland, one of the finest and bravest men I ever met. I had a good chance to get acquainted with him, as I was detailed, with nine others, as his body guard. Capt. Carr commanded one company of the First Dragoons; Maj. Plimton with a company of mounted infantry, and Company D of the Fourth United States Infantry.

We got on the trail and followed it up for three days and located the Indians in a Hummock where the underbrush was very thick, and it was very hard to push our way through it.

The command approached in two columns. The colonel, like the brave man that he was, led the way with his body guard in single file. When we got right onto the Indians I said: "Here they are, colonel," and I pulled my horse in front of the colonel. I had forgotten to mention that the body guard had been given horses when we started out. As I road in front of the colonel a very large Indian arose out of the bushes. I took deliberate aim and fired. The Indian jumped three feet in the air and fell dead. We advanced very rapidly and drove them into the heavy-timbered land, where we captured a part of the tribe, and in a few days got the rest of them; and I never saw a finer specimen of human physical perfection than were these people. Not at all like the stunted Indians who came from the western plains.

That night Col. Garland ordered me to Fort King with dispatches. That is about one hundred and ten miles from Tampa Bay. Warm springs are on the road about half the way from Tampa Bay to Fort King.

I left camp at twelve o'clock at night and got to Fort King some time in the forenoon next day. This was a big trip for my poor horse, for I weighed over a hundred and sixty pounds, and I carried my gun and equipments and one day's rations and forage for my horse. I had two rivers to ford, as the Indians had burned the bridges over the big and little Withlacoocha rivers. I also had several hummocks to cross. These are the dry lands which I spoke of before. Every rod of the way swarmed with rattlesnakes, moccasins and other deadly reptiles; besides part of the tribe was between me and Fort King. My horse was a spirited fellow and one used to the road, for he had born many an express rider over these very roads—some to the end of their journey and some were shot from his back, and their bones lay bleaching on the way and left monuments to American daring. I had little hopes of reaching Fort King. Every time we reached one of those dry hummocks my horse would prick up his ears and take the bit between his teeth, and no mortal man could hold him, but he dashed through like the brave, intelligent fellow that he was.

As soon as I learned his way I placed my leg over my gun to keep it from being brushed away and fastened my cap on my head and leaned over my horse's neck and let him go. Of course I could not see much of the road in the night, but much of the way was lit up by that brilliant Florida sunlight, and then the awful majestic grandness of that wild, fierce and many

times beautiful forest was aweinspiring, and must be
seen under such circumstances as I saw it to make
one fully understand it, for no pen, let it be wielded
by the best talent that ever scratched a line, could describe its impressive grandeur. Now, passing through
the swamps of low underbrush with a bare pathway,
which only my trusty horse could tread, for I knew it
not then, breaking over a space of dry land where a
road had been cut through, where the towering Magnolia, with its highly scented and beautiful blossoms,
perfumed the air for miles around, then the stately
palm nodded its proud head to the morning breezes,
while the live oaks yielded a comfortable shade from
the noonday glare of the sun and an equally fine
hiding place for a lurking foe.

The earth swarmed with poisonous insects and reptiles and the tops of the trees were fairly alive with
the most beautiful songsters I ever saw or heard. I
must take a little rest and a bite to eat and feed my
horse, so I seek a lonely spot on a lake shore; and
after we have taken a short rest, some food and drink
we are on our way again. But after daylight, with
the rather unpromising sights of dead men's bones
every little while to mark the way, it is no wonder my

hopes of a safe trip sank very low. But, of course, I got through safe.

Gen. Worth kept me at the fort two days before he started me on my return trip, and, as before, I started in the night and arrived back in camp safe the next day.

By this time our forces had captured the balance of the Indians. I had not been in camp but a few minutes when a squad of dragoons came to inquire if I had arrived safe, and if I had not, they intended to come out and meet me, as I had a very dangerous point to pass. It was about half way between Tampa Bay and Fort King, and at a point where Maj. Dade and one hundred and ten men were massacred on the 28th day of December, 1835. Maj. Dade had been ordered from Tampa to Fort King with supplies and ordinance, but a friendly chief went to Maj. Dade and told him of his danger and begged of him not to go, and told him just where his forces would be attacked; but Maj. Dade replied, saying: "There is no danger; I can drive every Indian out of Florida with a cowhide." The chief felt so bad that he shed tears, but it was no use. The major and his men left the next morning, taking one piece of artillery with them. They were three days before they reached the place where the massacre took place. They had arrived within one mile of the black cypress swamp when the twenty-five men on the advance guard were fired on, and Maj. Dade was the first to fall, and the whole advance guard were killed by the first fire. A fierce fight then ensued, but the Indians soon withdrew and the soldiers tried to build breastworks, but had not much done when the Indians came back with overwhelming numbers and renewed the fight.

There was no escape, every man but one being killed, and he was badly wounded, but managed to crawl to a lake and hide among the pond lilies. After the massacre the Indians terribly mutilated the bodies, and it was two weeks before they were buried. Then what could be found of the corpses were buried in one grave, and the cannon which the Indians had dismantled was placed at the head of the grave.

We now had the Indians of this section prisoners, except, perhaps, a few stragglers. We loaded them in wagons and took them to Tampa Bay. They were taken out to an island called Seehorsekees for safe keeping until a ship should arrive which was to take them to Fort Gibson, Indian Territory. There were several islands close by, and at low tide the Indians could wade from one to the other. So, to prevent them from escaping, there was a guard of ten men detailed to watch them. These islands swarmed with poisonous insects and reptiles. Comrade McDonough, a fine fellow, whom I liked very much, was one of the detailed guards. He laid down to sleep under a tree, and shortly after another comrade saw coiled on his chest a copperhead snake. The comrade was considering what to do when McDonough became restless and turned on his side, when the snake slid off and bit him on the forearm. It is said that no person ever recovered from the bite of a copperhead snake, and certainly I never heard of one who did except my friend McDonough, and this was on account of the presence of mind of the good comrade who saw the snake. He sprang to McDonough's side and applied his mouth to the wound and sucked the poison out, and McDonough recovered, showing but very little inconvenience from it.

A TERRIBLE TRAGEDY.

Kentucky acquired the title of "Dark and bloody ground," but during the Seminole war Florida wore an aspect fully as dark and terrible. Many were the massacres that drenched her soil and terrible were the tragedies that, if recorded, must blot the pages of history. But I will only mention those which came under my observation, or that I knew something about.

I was for a time stationed at a place called Wacahoota. This is about six miles from Macnope. Maj. Stanaford, in command of two companies of men, was at Macnope, and Maj. Graham, in command of two companies, was at Wacahoota. We had the best bread at our post, and so I was ordered every morning to take a basket of fresh bread over to Maj. Stanaford, who had his wife with him, so I became familiarly acquainted with them.

On one occasion Mrs. Montgomery, accompanied by the Sergeant-Major and an escort of five men, started to come over to Wacahoota, where Mrs. Montgomery wished to visit some friends. When half way between the two places they were attacked by the Indians, and after a bitter struggle all were killed. The sergeant-major and the lady were the last slain. When Lieut. Montgomery heard of the death of his wife, it crazed him, so he placed the point of his sword to his eye and fell upon it and killed himself.

Afterward a block house was built where the massacre took place, and was ever after guarded.

While stationed at Wacahotee, I, with nine others, were detailed to guard Maj. Hope's plantation against the depredations of thieving Indians. We were quartered at the major's house, and one man was kept on patrol continually night and day. This was performed in detail by each man going over the place and returning, which took him about two hours; then he was relieved by another. Thus the task was not a heavy one, but shows what varity we found in a soldier's life. While off duty, the time was spent in card playing or any way we could find to amuse ourselves. I was at this place about three weeks, when all at once I became

A DOCTOR.

This was a startling as well as an amusing and interesting episode of my life.

Dr. Hammond was our regimental surgeon, and a man by the name of Ben Rolet was hospital steward. Rolet was a good man and knew his duty well, was finely educated and perfectly competent for the work but for the one exception—he drank terribly, and so could not be trusted. Well, an orderly came to the plantation with orders for me to report to the hospital at once. Had I been ordered to report to the guardhouse and put under arrest, I could not have been more astonished. I should have thought that by some error I had been derelict in duty. Or had I been ordered to report to the commander, I would have supposed that I might be detailed for some special duty; but to be ordered to report to the doctor, and I not in need of medicine, certainly did puzzle me. My comrades joked me, saying that I might be a victim for vivisection as a live corpse, as it were, to be dissected for the benefit of future generations. But all of my imaginings were brought to an end when I reached the doctor's quarters. Said the doctor in his brusk way: "I have ordered you here to act as hospital steward." "But, doctor, I know absolutely nothing of medicine," said I. "I don't care a d——n for that. I will teach you," said he. I thought in my startled anxiety, for I did not want to be a doctor, I would declare I could not write. "Let me see your writing," said he. So I scratched down Baltimore or some other name in the most wretched manner I could, which was bad enough at best. He looked at it and said: "That will do." And so I was forced to become a doctor against my will. Well, after all it was not much, for the whole stock in trade of the pharmacy of a regimental hospital, in those days, was Peruvian bark in a powdered state. Its more powerful extract, quinine, calomel, laudanum, was a great stand-by in those days. Bitter aloes was much used, seidlitz powders, ipecac, jalap and, perhaps, the number of drugs could be counted on one's fingers, and did not take very long to learn their names, medical properties and quantities to be used, and the variety of diseases among soldiers was not so great. So I became quite a doctor in a little while. Bleeding and cupping were practiced a great deal, and I became so proficient in these that I was frequently called by the town people outside; and I made a good deal of extra money by my outside practice.

A GREAT JOKE ON DR. HAMMOND.

One night a man by the name of Collins, who had been a practicing physician, called at the surgery and asked for some laudanum. Knowing his previous record, I thought he could use his own judgment, and I said: "There it is; help yourself." But in a little while several men brought him back in a seemingly dying state. I immediately gave him a big dose of ipecac and tried all I could to bring him to. But he seemed so far gone that I called Dr. Hammond. But I did not tell him what ailed the man. He looked at the man and said: "Give him forty drops of laudanum." And he stood by until I administered the dose. But the moment his back was turned I poured down more ipecac. Meantime the old hospital steward, Rolet, came in, and I confided the truth of the matter to him. He helped me all he could, but the man was no better, and we called Dr. Hammond again, but did not tell him what the real trouble was. The doctor again looked at the sick man and said: "Repeat the dose; give him forty drops more laudanum." There was no escaping this, of course. It had to be done. But again we commenced our work of getting rid of it the moment the doctor's back was turned. Well, after a while we brought our man around all right. The next morning the doctor came in to the hospital accompanied by some friends and two other regimental doctors, and he brought them over to see the patient. "Now, this man," said he, "came in last night suffering from a severe attack of spinal mmeningitis. I ordered forty drops of laudanum, and as he did not make much progress I ordered the dose repeated, and here he is on a fair way to recovery. Only for the laudanum he would have died sure." And the other doctors stepped up and looked wise and nodded their heads as if to say, "Great wisdom; remarkable recovery." But of course we dare not let the "cat out of the bag," and the doctor never knew what really ailed the patient. But I tell you I was glad when Collins got well, and I was more watchful of my charge, the medicines, after that. Collins knew what he had taken, but he never gave the thing away.

DR. HAMMOND AND THE GERMAN MUSICIAN.

Dr. Hammond was a man of very few words and he was very gruff. One morning at sick call one of the band, a German musician by the name of Riter, reported for medical treatment. The doctor inquired, "What ails you?" "French horn, sir," replied Riter, supposing the doctor asked him what instrument he played. "D—n you!" shouted the doctor, "I did not want to know what instrument you played, but what is the matter with you." Finally the Dutchman got him to understand he had a pain in his stomach. But when Riter reported next morning and the doctor asked him "How is your chest?" he was completely knocked out by the Dutchman's reply, which was to the effect that some one had broken into it and stole a shirt and pair of drawers the night before, which was a fact. But the doctor did not know this, and supposed it was an attempted joke on him, and he kicked poor Riter out, crying, "D—n you, get out!"

A short time after this we were ordered to Jefferson barracks, Mo., about ten miles from St. Louis. We were ordered to pack the medicines in good shape, but so they could be easily got at in case of emergency. Dr. Hammond was in the habit of taking his seidlitz powders in the morning, and Rolet, knowing this, had determined to perpetrate one more joke on the doctor, knowing that at Jefferson barracks there was a fully equipped hospital department and he and I would be returned to the ranks, and as he had been ordered to assist in packing the medicines he was not at all particular, and more than likely mixed bitter allows with the seidlitz powders on purpose to perpetrate the joke. At any rate, while on board the boat going up the river, the doctor looked for his seidlitz powders, and at the first swallow made a terribly wry face and blurted out: "Who in h—l put bitter allows in my seidlitz powders?" "I dont know," I replied. "You ordered Rolet to pack the medicines, and he packed them." I had not better record exactly what the doctor said; it was not very complimentary to the hospital stewards and ended up with, "D—n the stewards; one is a d—n drunkard and the other is a d—n fool." Upon reaching Jefferson barracks we were returned to our companies. And so ended my experience as a doctor.

I will tell one more anecdote of our Florida campaign, and then I am done with that.

A DASTARDLY ACT.

With the Indians we captured at the battle of Douain was a colored boy fourteen years of age, and he said he was on board a vessel which was lost on the Florida coast. He with the captain and ten men were saved in a small boat and reached shore. They were standing under the bluff, when a voice called from above, "Come up here; we will not hurt you." The person spoke such good English that no one doubted but what everything was all right. But when they got up on the cliff they met a large band of Indians under Chief Tiger-tail, one of the most treacherous and bloodthirsty devils that ever lived. They pretended to be very friendly.

The captain had a very pretty bright new hatchet which the Indians admired, and the chief borrowed it, and each Indian went and cut a club with it, and when they had done this the chief spat on his hands as a signal and the Indians sprang on the white men and beat their brains out with the clubs. But they kept the boy, and his story was the first that was ever known of what became of the boat and crew.

AT JEFFERSON BARRACKS.

While at Jefferson barracks I was taken very sick with malarial fever, and while I took the doctor's medicine I believe Mother Earth did more for me than did the medicine, for every night I would steal out of my bed and go to a deep hole in the ground and lay there until cooled off and refreshed and then steal back again. I always believed that was what cured me. While I was in the hospital my company was ordered to Fort Scott, then Indian Territory, now Kansas. But I was not alone; there were five or six of us left behind and when we got well we were sent to join our command. A steamboat took us up the Missouri River as far as Boonville and the boat froze in. Col. Mason, of the First Dragoons, was on board the boat, and he told me to get a team and go to Fort Leavenworth, Kansas. He said he had some stuff to take up there and there would be plenty of room in the wagon for us after that. But after the wagon was loaded there was no room for us and we had to march. Well, we got along very well. Whenever we reached a stopping place for the night I would order whatever we required for men and team, and before we started away I would call for my bill and astonish the landlord by giving him an order on the quartermaster at Fort Leavenworth for his pay. It was useless to kick, for we were Uncle Sam's men, and the pay was sure though somewhat troublesome to collect; and it was a long time after our arrival that the bills were coming in and being promptly paid by the quartermaster.

We remained only a few days at Fort Leavenworth and then went on to Fort Scott. We were given a mule and cart and a man to drive to assist us on our way. On Christmas day, 1843, it snowed and rained all day, so that when we arrived at the crossing of the Merrydezine River the river had risen so we could not cross. We remained there a few days until the river lowered enough for us to cross, and then we pursued our journey. But this delay had not been counted on, and our rations ran out, and we were in the wilds without food. I took my gun and went in search of game. I took a trail and followed it for some distance when I was seized with a fit of

BUCK FEVER.

I had never hunted game bigger than a squirrel, and of course was rather a green hunter after larger game. I had not gone up the trail very far when a massive large buck deer met me face to face not ten feet away. I had heard something and was standing at order arms when he walked up to me and looked me square in the face. It took me so by surprise that I never thought of my gun loaded with ball and three buck-shot, and after he had looked me in the eye for a full minute he turned and bounded away. Had I had sense enough to shoot him it would have furnished us meat enough to last for some days. But we were now able to pursue our journey on the opposite side of the river.

This section of country came into our hands when France ceded Louisiana to the United States, and on the west side of the river it was quite thickly populated with French, descendants of De Soto, and it was chiefly owned by the American Fur Company. So after we crossed the river we were well taken care of until we reached Fort Scott. We found at Fort Scott two companies of artillery, two of infantry and two of the First Dragoons. They had built themselves very good winter quarters by hewing out logs and building log cabins.

DETAILED AS A CARPENTER.

There is always more or less carpenter work to be done around a fort and officers' quarters. Having worked some at carpenter work, I was detailed while at the fort on special duty as a carpenter. For this I received sixteen cents a day extra pay and a gill extra of whisky. But as I cared nothing for the whisky, I gave it to those who liked it better. But the extra pay came very good, for a private soldier's pay at that time was but seven dollars a month, clothing and rations; and the sixteen cents extra brought my pay up to eleven dollars and eighty cents per month. There was little of interest to note while here at Fort Scott; but I will relate two little incidents to show what may come into a soldier's life, and I will explain

HOW I BECAME A PUGILIST AGAINST MY WILL.

There are always some turbulent spirits among such a lot of men, who are ready to stir up a fuss, especially if they happen to get a little too much alcoholic spirits.

One day while at dinner, one of these soldiers of the turbulent spirit got into an altercation with a citizen, who gave him a deserved drubbing. But not as much as he ought to have. Of course I did not see the fracas and knew nothing of it until told me. But the turbulent comrade would not have it that way. He declared I saw it and would not come to his assistance. consequently was not a soldier if I would stand by and see a citizen pound a soldier. Denial of course was of no avail. But he insisted that I must go out and fight it out with him. Now I had no desire to fight, and, as he was a much larger man and a well known scrapper, it was worse than useless, I considered, trying my strength with him and I tried all I could to get out of it. But it stood this way: to flatly refuse to fight would be to be branded cowardly, and be the butt of every one's peccadillos who chose to pick on me, and to fight was to go out and take a pounding by a noted scrapper who bullied every one. I chose the latter. So we went out behind a cliff and had it out, and I tell you it was not all one-sided by any means. But I was like the Frenchman who got in trouble with the Yankee and they agreed that the one who felt whipped should cry enough and the other should stop. But the poor Frenchman, who was getting the worst of it, could not think of the word " enough," so he hollowed "Hurrah, hurrah," and the Yankee pounded the harder, until the poor Frenchman found something desperate was necessary and he put forth a mighty effort and turned his opponent and was drubbing him unmercifully when the Yankee cried "enough." "There," said the Frenchman, "That is what I was trying to think of a long time ago." But I tell you I was not in need of words. But my opponent had determined to give me a dreadful pounding and I stood it as long as I could, when I made a masterful effort and got the better of him, and he was taken to the hospital where he remained for several weeks until his time expired and he received his discharge. Then he came to me and showed me his buzzard, as he called his discharge, and said he laid nothing up against me, as I had given him the whipping he deserved and it would have made a man of him if he had received it sooner. He invited me to call on him if I ever came to Philadelphia and I should have the best the town could afford. But I never saw him afterward. But it was a great feather in my cap, for I was looked upon as the best man in camp after that. There was no places of amusement at Fort Scott, and the boys were compelled to rely on their own resources for amusement.

Some five miles out from the Fort was a place called Texas, a sort of frontier town. It consisted of a house divided into two parts, with a roof extending over a roadway between the two parts. It was from this place

I HAD A NARROW ESCAPE.

We were in the habit of going out there after taps, or the hour that the soldiers were supposed to be in bed asleep. Of course this means we were absent without leave. We would escape out of the barracks window, go out to this place and have a stag dance all night and get in before roll call in the morning. A squad of us from my company were favorites with the landlord, and as I played the flute it was a great help to the musical necessities for dancing. There was enough of our own crowd, and, consequently, if others were there they were advised to depart as the signal of our coming was wafted to the ears of the landlord through the notes of my flute as I played "Hail to the Chief." If the parties failed to take the advice of the landlord, a skirmish took place, and, to use a phrase of the times, the opposing parties were cleaned out. Of course, this was rather rough exercise and lent a rather tough name to the place.

Finally one night there was a check roll call and six of us reported absent without leave. So Major Graham sent a detachment of dragoons out there after us. I was the first to see the sabers at the door; I called to the boys and made a rush for the door. I leveled my flute like a gun and snapped the keys and shouted, "Get out of my way or I will blow your brains out." They were taken by surprise and I rushed by and ran all the way to camp and cleaned the mud off from my shoes and clothes, just in time for reveille and roll call.

The Orderly Sergeant said to me, "Jim, you was mighty sharp last night, but you look out next time."

The men afterward asked what kind of a gun I had that night. I laughed at them and told them it was no gun at all, but my flute, and they laughed heartily. But I was the only one who escaped. The other boys were punished by spending a month in the guard-house and losing a month's pay.

I had now served five years and my term of service had about expired and, having no place to call home, times were hard, and though the pay of a soldier—seven dollars a month, board and clothes, with some chances of extra pay—was small, yet the pay was sure and the money good; for the government never paid anything but gold and silver, and these were the days of scarcity of money, state bank notes, wild cat paper, store orders and trade, so a soldier's pay was not so bad after all. And I determined to reinlist. But I did not like to stay so far out on the frontier as Fort Scott was then, so I took my month's furlough and went to Jefferson Barracks, Mo., and reinlisted in Company F of the same regiment—the Fourth United States Infantry, Captain Page commanding. Captain Page was a personal friend of mine and I liked him very much, and afterwards mourned his death, for he was killed at Palo Alto, Texas, the first battle we got into.

HOW I BECAME A MUSICIAN.

I still clung to my flute, and often amused myself
with it while in my quarters. One day while practicing
the bandmaster chanced to be passing, and liking the
music so well, he came in and asked me how I would
like to join the band. I told him I would like it real
well. "Well," said he, "what instrument would you
like?" I replied that I would like the trombone. He
made application for my detail and had me reported
as learning music. I made such rapid progress that
in a very few days I was able to appear with the band
on guard mount. From this on music was my pride,
my aim and my profession, though I did some service
in the ranks after that. I was a member of the band
for ten years, thus making fifteen years of service in all.

We were at Jefferson barracks but a few months
when the whole regiment was ordered to a place
called Camp Salubrity, near Natchitoches, Louisiana,
presumably to be near the seat of war should war be
declared between the United States and Mexico, which
seemed quite imminent. We here built ourselves nice
quarters of logs, and were here for some months, and

then joined the army of occupation and took our position at Corpus Christi, Texas, Col. Twigs in command of the post. This was the same Twigs who went out of the Union and fought against our flag at the surrender of Fort Sumpter by Major Anderson, at the beginning of the Rebellion in 1861.

We were encamped close to the sea and it was a beautiful place. Here we had many places of amusement. We had a large billiard room and other features of comfort, and we built two theaters—"The Army" and "The Union." They were of course temporary, being frame structures with mere clabboard sides and covered with canvas. I played the trombone in the orchestra of the Union Theater.

We had about three thousand five hundred men in camp. Here I was appointed drum major and had both the band and field music in charge, so I continued playing in the band and directing both branches of music from that position.

We left Corpus Christi some time in April and took up our line of march for the Rio Grande River, a few days afterward arriving opposite to Matamoras. Santa Anna, the Mexican general, sent dispatches to Gen. Taylor to leave in twenty-four hours. Gen. Taylor replied that they were United States soldiers and had come to stay. Thus opened the

MEXICAN WAR,

which had been fomenting for some time. And war was not declared until May 26th, 1846.

At this place of occupation we built a very formidable fort and christened it Fort Taylor. Shortly after the Fort was completed Gen. Taylor left Major Brown in command with a force of five hundred men, and with the remainder of the army took up a line of march to Point Isabell, a station on the Gulf of Mexico, where we had our supplies.

Though I was drum major at this time, Col. Garland sent for me and said, "Mr. Elderkin, we are about to take up our line of march to Point Isabell. The Mexicans have crossed the river and we are going to have a fight and I wish you would take the colors of the regiment and carry them into Mexico." I thanked him for the honor conferred upon me and told him that the colors should never be disgraced in my hands, and I kept my word and was the first man to carry the American colors on to Mexican soil.

When we left Fort Taylor, we went in light marching order, merely taking two days' rations with us, and left our knapsacks in the fort, and it was well we did, for the Mexicans attacked us in great numbers and with artillery, and our men were compelled to use the army baggage to build a bomb proof for protection So our knapsacks were literally shot to pieces and we drew new knapsacks and clothing right away; and we all felt well satisfied so long as our clothing saved the lives of so many of our comrades.

The above statement can be found in Bancroft's History.

BATTLE OF PALO ALTO, MAY 8, 1846.

This occurred on the 8th and 9th of May, 1846. Maj. Brown was wounded at Fort Brown. The name of Fort Taylor was changed to Fort Brown.

As I say, we had taken nothing with us but two days' rations. We had no protection from the damp earth at night or nothing to cover us but the vault of the heavens.

After we arrived at Point Isabell we could hear the fighting at Fort Taylor. It took us two days to march from Fort Taylor to Point Isabell. We could make no fires, as that would expose our position.

On May the 9th we fought the battle of Reseca de la Palma. Here I made an important capture. We came upon the Mexicans so sudden we surprised them and they left a good dinner all cooked and of course we helped ourselves. And it fell to my good luck to get into the quarters of the Mexican Generals Leviga and Arista, whom we captured, and though I did not capture the generals I did capture a good dinner of soup, boiled beef and other eatables, also several boxes of fine cigars and a box of claret wine, and a box of chocolate. These luxuries were a great prize to a tired, hungry soldier who had subsisted on fat pork and hardtack and even without that for hours.

We did not cross over to Matamoras until the next day. We stopped here for several days and after we crossed over, some of the men found the body of Lieut. Porter, who had been killed by a Mexican citizen, or guerillas or Greaser, as they were more generally called. I was ordered to take the body back to Point Isabell to be sent to his friends.

Here I found my own dear old commander, Capt. Page, of my company, who had been badly wounded at the battle of Palo Alto. A piece of shell carried away the captain's lower jaw and took off the top of a private soldier's head. The soldier's name was Lee.

The army was now called the Army of Invasion. While we were at Matamoras I was taken very sick with congestive fever, and came very near dying. In those days we had no hospital nurses, not even cots for the sick and wounded; had nothing but a mere rush mat thrown on the ground.

Dr. Brown was the army physician who attended me and he afterward told me he did not expect I would recover, and sent a priest to come and pray for me. In those days doctors would not allow a drop of cold water in any case of fever. But as it was not thought I could live and as I was begging for cold water, the attendant was told to give me all the cold water I wished for; so they would bring in a large pan of water and after drinking all I wanted, I would hold one side of my head in it and then the other, and it helped me so much I was well in a few days and Dr. Brown told me afterward he learned a good lesson, and that was to give a fever patient all the cold water he wanted.

From Matamoras we took boats and went up the Rio Grande as far as it was navigable to a little place called Camargo; it was a very sickly place on the Rio Grande, about one hundred and fifty miles from its mouth. We lost many men here from disease and called the place Camp Graveyard. The army was here largely reinforced. And we marched on to Monterey. History records the gallant deeds of our noble army at this place.

The army was now divided into two invading armies. One to operate in the north, the other to operate in the south. My regiment, the Fourth U. S. Infantry, was transferred from Taylor's to General Scott's command and we again went down the Rio Grande to the Brasso, at its mouth, where we took ship for Vera Cruz.

The ships, of course, were merchantment, with rough accommodations for the men, hastily put in, and consisted of bunks built up, below the decks. These were built of green hemlock lumber, three tiers high; and on going to bed we were not allowed lights, so had to feel our way.

We were ten days on board, and our food was fat pork, hardtack, beans and rice. The water we had to drink was as vile as if dipped from a stagnant goose pond. The doctor ordered a gill of vinegar to each man, per day, to put in the water he drank. This made a little improvement, but not much. We went below the city about twelve miles, and when all of the ships arrived we sailed for the city, each boat towing its small boats behind. When we got near the beach close to the city, the men clambered over the ship's sides into the small boats, and as the small boats would ground before reaching shore, the men would jump into the sea and wade to shore.

The army disembarked with little trouble and were not molested until night, when the Mexicans attacked our pickets several times during the night. We immediately began building earthworks for protection, and for positions to plant our siege guns. The Mexicans evidently made a mistake in supposing we were going to attack the castle of San Juan Delhia, and they did not discover their error until we were too well fortified to be dislodged. We were now within a few hundred yards of the city, and continually advancing nearer. Each night a body of men would go out and work all night and be relieved the next night, while a detail of soldiers would go out to protect the fatigue party while at work. The doctor, with instruments and medicines, was on the line and the musicians in attendance with stretchers to carry the wounded off the field and to assist the doctor. I was with the doctor one day and Col. Garland sent for me, and asked me if I would volunteer to carry dispatches over to Gen. Worth. Of course I complied, though the way was over an exposed position and over a hill with not a thing to shelter a man from the Mexican fire. Said the colonel, "Now don't go stalking along as straight as an arrow as if you had a ramrod thrust down your back to keep it stiff; bend over and conceal yourself as much as possible, and pick your way without attracting any more attention than you can help; and you need not expose yourself by coming back. Stay in camp."

The city was one side of the hill, of course, and the line of advance between the hill and the city.

Let me here call the attention of the reader to the difference of the arms of those days and to-day. Remember there were no Gatling guns or machine guns of any kind. No, nor breech-loading guns of any kind, not even the oldest style of revolvers. Nothing but old flint-lock muskets for small arms and the artillery was very crude and short range, so two armies must come very close together before they could do any effective work.

The caliber of both musket and cannon was very large, and the cannon were little more than explosive catapults, throwing gigantic shells, that could be seen by the naked eye as hurled through the air.

When I was well up on the hill I thought I would look back and see the city and I turned around; I saw a puff of smoke, a great black object came flying toward me, and a shell of monstrous proportions, at least as large as a water pail, burst over my head. None of the pieces hit me, but the concussion was so great that it made me very deaf for days after that.

I was no longer courageous to see the city, but got on the other side of the hill as quickly as possible.

With our sharpshooters of to-day no man could ever get across such a place.

I am now seventy-eight years old and I naturally feel it is the goodness of God which has preserved my health and memory, so that all the events of my life from boyhood days are as fresh in my memory as those of years ago. I feel that God has been good

to me and I feel very thankful to God for all he has
done for me.

RAPID WORK.

Let it be remembered I told you General Taylor
had defeated and captured General Arista at the battle of Palo Alto, May 8th, 1846, and the battle of
Reseca de la Palma, May 9th, and after this, in the
same month, both governments declared war.

May 18th, General Taylor captured Matamoras, and
on September 24th he captured Monterey.

By casualties, with details of posts of occupation
and number of men General Scott had drawn from
Taylor's command, it left Taylor with but five thousand men, and with this small number he met and
defeated Santa Anna at Buena Vista with twenty-two
thousand men February 23d, 1847.

We had in our army under General Scott but ten
thousand men to meet Santa Anna with thirty thousand. But we were successful and captured Vera
Cruz March 18th, 1847.

The advance pursued the retreating Mexicans, and
as soon as the main army had rallied and reorganized
it followed closely on to the advance and we fought

the battle of Cero Gardo April 25th; San Antonio
and Canteerus, and Cherusbusco, August 20th; Molino del Rey, September 8th, and Chapultepec, September 13th, and on September 14th, 1847, we entered the City of Mexico, the Mexican capital. This
ended the fighting, but we remained the army of occupation until the treaty of peace was concluded on the
2d of February, 1848. This, of course, necessitated
very rapid movements and quick work and active
campaigning. Yet we had time to note the peculiari-
ties of the country and familiarizing ourselves with
many of its customs and conditions. Just before the
battle of Cero Gardo we spent a few days at the City
of Jalapa; this is a beautiful city of thirty thousand
population and is four thousand three hundred and
forty feet above the sea level. It is a favorite resort
for invalids. Puebla is another beautiful city still
higher up, and so high at this point that when people
first arrive in the city they begin to expand on account of the rarefied air, and their clothing though
loose before, soon becomes so tight as to be uncomfortable. It at first frightened our soldiers, for they
thought they were about to be attacked by some terrible disease, as the change brought on a slight diar-

rhoea and much bloating and wind. But the doctor assured the men that it was not a dangerous attack and they would soon find themselves better for the change, which was true. The climate here is very fine and notwithstanding the high altitude I never saw a flake of snow, except as we looked away to the top of the great volcanic mountain of Orizabo, which towers eighteen thousand feet above the sea level. Here on that mountain, snow could be seen the year around.

It was while at Jalapa I learned to speak the Spanish language, and I think it the sweetest sounding language in the world.

These Mexican cities, in their strange and picturesque beauty are indescribable. They all have beautiful parks with numerous cascade fountains, where the clear sparkling water comes gurgling and gushing from the mouths of dragons and serpents, and other strange designs, or dashing over miniature precipices. The parks are also thickly studded with a magnificent foliage of many varieties, including giant trees of immense height and from four to six feet in diameter at the butt.

Cero Gardo is a very strange position high in the mountain. A great plateau of table land with giant precipices here, and towering ledges of rock there, standing askew as if nature, when the earth was cooling from a molten mass, had wrenched the earth asunder, grasping and tearing out a huge proportion and carrying it away to leave a shelf where man might get a foothold and build his habitation. It was here in this strange place we captured General Santa Anna's carriage, his wooden leg and a large box of Mexican dollars. We also captured forty pieces of artillery and seven thousand prisoners.

Such arms and property we could not remove was consigned to flames and destroyed and the prisoners paroled.

While at Jalapa, we took a very strong fort called Perota Castle, situated on a plain where it can be seen for a great distance. Here we found great dungeons and confined in them the desperate characters of Mexico. We found confined here the notorious Mexican bandit, Captain Camiloes, I believe was his name, and a large number of his men. The leader promised General Scott that if he would liberate them, they would serve and be true to this country as long as the war lasted. They were liberated and the leader given a colonel's commission in our army, over his own men, of course, and they acted as scouts, and General Scott procured information in this way he could have procured in no other way. But these were as bloodthirsty a lot of devils as ever lived; the captain had perfect control over them, but he was as merciless as the rest. On one occasion they met a Spanish nobleman with his daughter. They killed the father, and one of the men insulted the young girl when the leader or colonel shot him dead. Such was their peculiar sense of justice and honor.

Concentress was the only battle mentioned in which I was not engaged in in General Scott's campaign. It was taken very quickly, early in the morning, by Colonel Riley's forces. At the battle of Cherubusco Michigan lost some men from the First Michigan Infantry, one of whom's name was William Cunningham. Sergeant Cunningham went from Detroit. His wife was a sister to my wife, though at this time I was not married and never knew him. He was in the same regiment with the late Colonel W. D. Wilkins, of Detroit, who afterward was long identified with the Detroit Light Guards.

At the beginning of the war the Mexican government offered great inducements to deserters of the American army. To those capable of taking command they offered commissions and to all great land bounties, and other inducements. As there were quite a number of adventurers, or wanderers from all nations in our army—men who considered no particular country their home, many of them became dazzled by these offers, and deserted and joined the Mexicans.

After we got possession of a fort that commanded a bridge going into Cherubusco, there was firing from a church, about a hundred yards from the fort. As it overlooked our position we could not see the firing parties, while they were picking off our men rapidly. Colonel Garland ordered up a piece of captured artillery and brought it to bear on the church. As soon as the parties in the church saw the uselessness of farther resistance they displayed a white flag. They came into the fort and threw down their arms, and the officer approached Colonel Garland and said: "If you treat us as prisoners of war we will not take up arms against the United States as long as the war lasts." There were sixty of them. All were recognized as deserters, some having deserted at Fort Brown and

others later on. They were all tried by court martial
and sentenced to be hung. The sentence was executed on all but one, Colonel Riley, who escaped with
the punishment of being branded on the left cheek
with the letter D—deserter. It was placed in the
hands of General Harney to see the decision of the
court martial should be carried into effect. He was
the same rough old Indian fighter known as the
"Squaw Killer," from his killing a squaw who attacked him, and his ordering the men to fire on the
squaws as well as the men. On the morning of the
execution one of the prisoners was reported too sick
to be brought out. But the old general said: "Bring
him out and hang him; d——n him, that will cure
him."

After leaving Cherubusco we crossed a bridge and
went to a small place, called Tuckeybia. It is only
three miles from the city of Mexico, and near this
was a place of importance for us to take called Molino
del Ray. Here was a fort of stone built in the middle
of the road, called in English, King's Mills. This was
only about three hundred yards from the Castle of
Chapultepec. The night before the battle we had
orders to remain under arms all night. Early in the

morning we commenced to move toward King's Mills. I was back in my position with the band again and I did not like to stay behind so I tried to get a musket, but the extra guns were in the wagons and I could get none. So I went to Major Lee and told him I wanted to go with the regiment and asked him what I should do. Said he: "You can act as my orderly," as he was in command of the regiment, Colonel Garland then being in command of the brigade. We had been under arms all night and without a moment's sleep, so we were well night fatigued out; we moved close to the fort, before daylight, and laid down and at the first blast of their bugle for reveille, we charged the works, at first covered by artillery which consisted of four light batteries, Ringold, Duncan, Stepto and McGruder in command. The horses were sent to the rear and the men shoved the artillery up before them and fired as they went.

This was the hottest engagement I ever experienced. The balls came so thick one could not help feeling like putting his hand before his face as if it were hail, yet we kept so close to the ground that we escaped most of the damage we otherwise must have received. But as it was we lost many men, and among them

Lieut. Prince, of my regiment. He was the man who enlisted me at Schenectady, N. Y., in 1839. He was shot in the thigh, and I carried him into a house close by.

The next day we had to take Chapultepec; this is a castle only three miles from the city of Mexico. And as the streets were blocked and batteries so placed to sweep the streets, our men were compelled to go through the houses, knocking down walls and so cutting our way through from house to house. But before we reached this point of attack we laid siege to the castle for several days. We had large siege guns and mortars placed and bombarded it until we were ready to make the assault.

One day I went down to see the working of the guns while bombarding, and while I was at the fort they fired one of the pieces. I chanced to be a little in the advance of the piece though not in range, of course, but quite sufficient to give me a terrible shock and nearly deafened me for a time. I noticed a man near the gates of the castle on horseback, and when the shell burst it killed man and horse, blowing them all to pieces.

The day we stormed the stronghold I would not remain in the rear with the band but got a gun from the Eighth Infantry, and fell in with the storming party. We were provided with rope ladders with hooks attached; these we would throw up and grapple the top of the wall and climb up and throw the ladder over and descend on the other side. Of course there was hard fighting to prevent our entrance. Here a Mexican officer attempted to prevent my descending from the wall and I was compelled to shoot him. This terrible thing grew into a deed of gallantry and I have still in my possession a Record of Merit given me by President James K. Polk for this day's work. I now fell in with Company C of my regiment and Orderly Sergeant Shadly, who was in command of the company, told me to take his place at the right of the company; I did so and stayed with them for some time. We were now following the Mexicans right up to the gates of the city of Mexico.

They had erected a number of forts in the streets and it was hard fighting as we advanced and drove them before us. After turning a bend in the road I noticed some Mexicans industriously firing at our men; I took deliberate aim and fired, and although

they were two hundred yards away I wounded one
of them, and we soon drove them out and I captured
the one I had wounded. General U. S. Grant was
then captain and was quartermaster. Chancing to see
him I took my prisoner to him. Captain Grant told
me to break his gun and let him go, which I did.
This squad of men were guarding a Spanish gentleman's home; when I came up to the house the old
gentleman was terribly frightened, and he came out
with his sixteen-year-old daughter on one arm and
with the other hand extended he held a bag of gold.
I told him, in the best Spanish I could command, that
I was a soldier and not a robber. Yet I must say I
started out with some idea that I might gather in
some wealth; but when I saw that poor old man with
his pretty daughter on his arm and half-scared to
death and begging for mercy, I could not have
touched his gold. But alas, poor old man, he made
the mistake of supposing all would serve him the
same as I did, but the next man who came up took
the proferred bag of gold, and, I was told, the bag
contained seven thousand dollars in doubloons, and I
have often thought I might as well have had it as
the other fellow. Just at this time Captain Grant,

who had left his trusty assistant, Sam Smith, in charge
of the quartermaster's department, and was at the
front for business, called for volunteers from a lot of
men who seemed to be fighting on their own hook as
it were, and as the captain was doing the same thing,
he called about thirty of them together, and I joined
the crowd, and we followed along down the side of
the aqueduct which supplies the city of Mexico with
water, to a little fort which Captain Grant and his
forces captured. We held this until relieved by other
advancing forces. When Captain Grant tried to dis-
lodge another body of men who were doing our forces
much damage. But we could not get at them; in
some way Captain Grant got a small piece of artillery,
and we took it on top of a house and fired there.
Under the protection of this gun the men cut their
way from house to house, and thus drove the enemy
before us. Our loss was very small in comparison
to what it would have been had we tried to advance
up the road. In passing through the houses in this
way, it offered great inducements for plunder. But
the ridiculousness of a soldier bothering with plunder
may be readily seen when you consider we were hundreds of miles in the interior of an enemy's country,

with no means of transporting food while we marched out of it, much less to transport plunder. Yet there were some so foolish as to attempt to take plunder. One foolish fellow came out of one of the houses with a large bundle of silk dresses and such stuff. He attempted to cross the street when he was wounded by a grape shot striking him in the leg. He dropped to the earth and cooly put the bundle under his head. Several times our men tried to save him, but were driven back, so he was left to his fate, which was of short duration, for another shot hit him in the head and ended his career.

By this time we had been fighting all day, and arrived at the gates of the City of Mexico.

I must here state, for the benefit of those not familiar with the history of Mexico, that the old City of Mexico was walled in, but it had expanded beyond the walls.

As I was standing, looking around, Captain Grant approached leading a mule. He said to me, "Here is a nice mule; you can have it if you want it." I took the mule and thanked him, and lead the mule over to where I intended to stop for the night, and tied it to a tree, and that was the last I ever saw of it.

For that night the city was surrendered, and we were to take possession in the morning.. So amid the excitement and hurry some one else lead the mule away. The next morning we entered the city with much pomp and parade.

General Scott was a very large man, six foot six in hight, and built in proportion, and he rode a very large and magnificient horse. Wearing a bright uniform with a large hat and feather, he was a wonderful sight to see.

The whole army had slicked up as much as possible, and a proud general and a proud army it was; and it had a right to be proud after so long a march, and fighting so many battles without loosing a battle. The bands were playing and flags flying, pomp, parade and show. We were even welcomed by many Mexicans. But there were some who tried to welcome us too warmly, and notwithstanding the official surrender of the city, they fired on us from some of the houses.

General Scott then gave the order to the provost guards to enter houses where firing took place and kill every inmate regardless of sex or age. But the only case where I ever heard of the thing being done was a case where a lieutenant saw some men firing, and he got a lot of armed teamsters together and captured the men, and took them all out and placed them up beside a stone wall, and gave the order, "Make ready, take aim, fire;" I believe fifteen fell dead.

After entering the City of Mexico many strange things took place. Saloons were thrown open, liquor was plenty, and some heedless men drank until intoxicated, and dropped to sleep wherever they chanced to be. Alas, poor fellows, many of them slept their last sleep, for as soon as found alone and helpless the Mexicans would cut their throats. I saw one of our own men fall to sleep intoxicated. I passed on and opened the faucets and let the liquor run away to keep it from the men, and on turning back a few moments afterward I saw this poor fellow's throat was cut from ear to ear.

Shortly after we entered the city the Mexican Bandit Scouts, freed, and employed by General Scott, went to the Mexican mint and helped themselves; one of our men by the name of Dan Carr, a drummer, went with them, and he filled his haversack with the bright coin and brought it to camp.

I will here relate a few incidents of war, and which still come up fresh in my memory. Every reader of history will quickly recognize the name of

GENERAL PHIL. KERNEY.

I knew General Kerney well when he was a lieutenant in the Dragoons, and a more courageous man never lived, but he was very eccentric. He loved a beautiful horse and a fine looking soldier above everything else on earth. He was very wealthy, and if he saw an uncommon fine appearing young soldier who kept everything neat and clean, he would often stop him and compliment him on his soldierly appearance, and perhaps give him several dollars in money. If there was anything new in saddles or equipments came up and the government was slow in adopting them, Kerney would equip his company with them at his own expense. He always had several very fine horses, and on one occasion, just before the Mexican war, we were in camp at Fort Gibson. The lieutenant was slicking up his quarters and whitewashing stables when one of the men asked him what he should white-wash. The lieutenant replied, "Whitewash everything, d—n it." Now the lieutenant had one beautiful black horse he thought everything of, and as the men had been roughly told to whitewash everything, they, for mischief, whitewashed the horse. When Kerney came out and saw the horse he said to his servant, "Andrew, what d—n fool has put that horse in here; what horse is it?" The servant, finally recognizing the horse, said, "It is your horse, lieut." "It is no such a d—n thing, it is not my horse, turn him out." Strange to say, this eccentric man would never have anything to do with or claim the horse after that; it had been disgraced.

The first U. S. Dragoons was the finest body of men I ever saw. Their uniforms were beautiful black jackets, a straight hat, from which waved long and beautiful black plumes. Horses the best that Uncle Sam could provide for them. When they rode in line, wheeled and maneuvered at the sound of the bugle, it was a sight to inspire any man with enthusiasm and pride.

Lieutenant Kerney with his company charged on the gates of the City of Mexico, and it was in this gallant charge that the lieutenant lost his arm.

MY FIRST EXPERIENCE WITH AN EARTH-QUAKE.

While we were in the city, the band occupied the upper floors of a large building. We were expected to leave the city at any moment.

One morning, about nine o'clock, I was getting ready for guard mount, and while putting on my sash I felt a reeling sensation as if I could not keep my feet, and was about to say to the men, I will not be able to go on duty, when I looked up and saw a crack in the roof and walls of the building. I told the men to get out of the building as quickly as possible.

Mr. Flair, a Mexican veteran and member of the band, declared I was excited, and said, "Get out, get out of this, you devils, get out of this." I was no doubt excited some, and remember distinctly what I said, and that I told the men to get down out of the building as quickly as possible. Well might a person feel sick and excited, for when we reached the street the houses seemed to be dancing a reel. I had an experience of this kind in California afterward.

A STRANGE WAY OF SUBSISTING AN ARMY.

Perhaps in no other case is it recorded in history where an invading army, by treaty, purchased its supplies of the country invaded. But such was the case here. There was an armistice called, and General Scott made arrangements with the Mexican Government that we might purchase our supplies of them; so we would send a wagon train, under guard and flag of truce, to the gates of the City of Mexico, and a Mexican guard would take them and return the wagons filled with flour, beans, sugar, coffee, bacon and other eatables and forage for the teams.

This arrangement was very fortunate, as it saved us from transporting the stuff, by teams, over a hundred miles from Vera Cruz, or from robbing the inhabitants, and thus making more bitter foes; so in this way we only had the army and not an outraged public to fight.

WE LEAVE MEXICO.

The war over, and peace declared, the invading army must now leave Mexico, so we marched back to Tuckeybia and halted a few days, and then went to Vera Cruz, where ships were awaiting us. Our march was hurried, so the ships would not have long to wait, and consequently we were very fatigued. But we were all anxious to get on board ship so as to get home as soon as possible. Our native land seemed more dear to us than ever before, as we had been absent in an enemy's country for two years. Although our experience was a varied one and not entirely void of passing interest and pleasure.

We found the ships in a much better condition on our return than those in which we came. Such comforts could not last long, and we were but a few days on board ship when we arrived at Pascagoula camp. near New Orleans, a little ways from Mobile Bay. This camp was called Camp Jefferson Davis, after the name of the Secretary of War, who was afterward President of the Southern Confederacy. It was a very pretty place, a resort for New Orleans people during

the sickly season. We had the best of dramatic talent
in our regiment, and we built a theater so we could
use it and amuse ourselves. General Taylor came
here to visit us, and we gave him a picnic at an island
a short distance away. But here again, it seemed to
be too nice a place, and we did not stay long, but
went from here to New Orleans. Here we went on
board an old ship the government had purchased to
take us to New York. But she was a rotten old thing
and had no accommodations. No bunks, or even any
way of cooking, so we were compelled to live on hard
tack and raw salt pork. We were compelled to sleep
below, and around on the floor, or wherever we could
find a place. Every reel of the old tub would bring
the sea water down the hatches and wet the men.

After we left the mouth of the Mississippi, a terrible
storm came up and played the deuce with us. The
ship lost her rudder, and sustained other damages, and
left us at the mercy of the waves, and for three days
we were tossed about and no one thought it was possible for us to ever reach safety. But Divine destiny
had decreed differently.

The fourth morning a calm came over the face of
the waters. The sun shone bright and clear, not a

cloud to be seen, and it seemed to me we had risen right out of the sea. While the storm lasted we were engulfed in the ocean, seemingly with walls of water on every side; but now it seemed as if we had risen high above it.

About ten o'clock we could see smoke a great distance away. The captain said they had discovered our signal and came to our rescue. A tremendous cheer went up from the men when the announcement was made. The smoke we saw came from a tug boat out in search of wrecks. The tug towed us back to New Orleans. We were now put aboard the steamer Crescent City, a very fine boat, and once more started for New York. But again we were destined for trouble. The pilot who was assigned to take us out had bad eyesight and ran us aground, near the mouth of the river, and we were compelled to stay there for five days and to unload her cargo, and then it took four tugs and much hard swearing to get her off. After this we had no more trouble, but went straight to Havana, Cuba. We passed right under the walls of Morro Castle and went into the harbor. We stayed here for five days, and enjoyed it very much. I was favorably impressed with Havana at that time.

I listened to some of the finest music I ever heard. They had two of as fine bands there as I have ever had the pleasure of listening to. The band that played at the Governor-General's Palace was one hundred pieces strong, and they played every night for two hours. The air was full of music all of the time.

After leaving Havana we pressed on to New York. We put in at Wilmington, North Carolina, and stayed for five days, and again pursued our course.

Nothing happened to disturb us and we arrived in New York all right. We here reshipped and went to Albany, N. Y. We were here put upon all sorts of box and freight cars and started for Buffalo. We made a number of stops on the way so the men could get coffee, and warm meals. At Buffalo we took the boat for

DETROIT.

When we arrived in Detroit, November 17, 1848, Detroit, Michigan, was a very small place. The city had no more than ten thousand inhabitants at that time. We were quartered in a barracks which occupied the ground where the Arbeiter Hall now stands, at the corner of Catherine and Russell streets. The barracks and grounds took in the whole space now bounded on the south by Catherine street, on the north by Gratiot, on the east by Russell and on the west by Rivard street.

The grounds of the Municipal building, where the Police and Recorder's Courts are held, was then the city's burying grounds. There were no pavements and very few sidewalks in the city. The soldiers built a lengthwise and three-plank wide sidewalk from the barracks down to Jefferson avenue, so we could march down to church corner Woodward avenue and Woodbridge street. Nearly all of the way to Jefferson avenue was commons; in fact, from Beaubien street east and from the river to Catherine street was commons, swarming with plover, which made fine shooting for the sportsman. East and north of the barracks was very much heavy timbered land.

We had been in Detroit some time when two of my brothers, hearing I was in Detroit, came to see me. This was the first time I had seen any of my folks since I left my brothers' place so abruptly thirteen years before. I went with them, to their homes down in Ohio, and stayed for some time, and when my furlough expired returned to the company.

The regimental band and two companies only were stationed here, the rest of the Fourth U. S. Infantry were placed as follows: Mackinaw, Fort Gratiot,

Oswego, Platsburgh and Niagara and Sault de Ste. Marie.

Captain U. S. Grant, the late President Grant, was in command here. His residence was on Fort street east. I now pass the house nearly every day. Captain Grant was very friendly to me, and I used to take his mail down to his house every day, and it was on one of these trips I met my fate, and here comes the

LOVE STORY

of my life. Up to a couple of years ago there stood an old building, on the south side of Catherine street near Russell, where lived a German family by the name of Bessinger. As I passed the house one morning I saw a beautiful dark-eyed young girl training some vines; they were laden with beautiful flowers, and she in her youthful beauty looked to me more like a beautiful flower than all of the rest.

I asked her the name of the flower she seemed to be admiring, and she said, "It is a morning glory." "Well," said I, "then you must be an evening beauty." After this I managed to call her attention every time I passed that way; and I am afraid I passed quite frequent, for our friendship soon ripened into a first class love match. But this did not quite suit her mother, for this girl was little more than a child and

TAKEN AT SACKETT'S HARBOR, N. Y., 1851 (FROM
DAGUERREOTYPE).

the youngest and the pet of the family, and the mother
said, "I have already two daughters who married
soldiers, and you must not go and leave me." But
young love knows no laws, locksmiths or language
they can allow to baffle, or hinder them, so it was
soon arranged, and a little girl, a friend, would call
on Mary and take her out for a walk, and of course
they always knew just where to find me. But this
dodging and stolen opportunities seemed too much
of a hardship and we determined to get married. So
when I got everything ready, George Harron, who is
still in the city, came with his carriage, and was in
waiting when she slided out to meet me. We jumped
into the carriage and were driven to Justice Wilker's
house. He performed the marriage ceremony, and his
wife was one of the witnesses and Sergeant Burgan
was the other. It was this way I met and married
my dear wife, the noble woman, who with ever watchful care, like a ministering angel, hovered over me
when ill or anticipated my daily wants, and counseled
with me, thus following my fortunes, through long
and wearied travel and on the tented field or in my
city home, where the peaceful pursuits made the quiet
and happiness of home life possible. She died July

18th, 1888. Therefore nearly forty years of wedded bliss smoothed over many of the rough spots in seventy-eight years of rugged life.

As soon as the marriage ceremony was performed we returned to the barracks, and I found a boarding place for my wife across the street from the barracks on Russell street. Afterward I had a place prepared for her at the barracks.

I was financially very short at this time, but I had many friends who stood ready to assist me. I was thirty years old at this time and she sixteen; thus it will be seen I was fourteen years older than my wife.

I reinlisted in Detroit for five years, making fifteen years' service in the United States Regular Army. We were in Detroit a little over a year when the two companies here were ordered to Sackett's Harbor, New York, where we remained one year, when we got orders to California. While we were stationed at Sackett's Harbor Lieutenant McConnel was adjutant of the regiment, but was absent from the post for a few days, and Captain U. S. Grant was acting in his place.

I had a drummer in the band by the name of Herman. Herman was a very good man, and a good drummer, but he had one great failing. He drank too much whisky for his own good. Furthermore, he was continually absenting himself when he had duty to perform. I had frequently reprimanded him for this, and the very day before the following event I told him if he did not attend to his duty better in the future I would be compelled to make a complaint against him. But the next evening when it was time to beat the tatoo he was absent. He came about ten minutes late. I said nothing to him until after tatoo, and then I went to him and told him to go get his blanket, as I was going to put him in the guard house. He showed his resentment by assailing me; but I was too quick for him and was compelled to knock him down. After he came to he set up a terrible howl, and the officers all came out of their quarters to see what was the matter. I took him to the guard house and then reported the matter to Captain Grant. I also told him I had some dangerous men, who, when intoxicated, would resent arrest with personal violence, and that my orders were not to strike a man. Said he, "Who gave you that order?" Said I, "Adjutant McConnel." "Well, I tell you, if a man resists arrest, knock him down."

Adjutant McConnel was a good man and a fine officer, but he was not the prompt disciplinarian that Captain Grant showed himself to be.

While at this post the band spent two weeks at each of the different posts where the other companies of the regiment were stopping, Sault Ste. Marie, Mackinaw, Fort Gratiot, Oswego, Platsburgh and Niagara. At all of these places our music was appreciated and we were well received by the comrades and citizens.

The leader of our band at this time was a fine musician, as well as a gentleman. He was a Prussian by birth, and had served in the Prussian army. He enlisted in Detroit some time before we went to Sackett's Harbor. Prior to his enlistment we had a band leader by the name of Hess; he also was a German, but was considered by officers as a back number, and they desired to get a leader more modern. Though Mr. Hess was a good old gentleman, he was a wheezy, stuffey old man, always with a snuff box in his hand, and almost filthy in appearance. But when he enlisted good musicians were hard to get, and he was very important and would not enlist unless allowed to resign whenever he wished to, and this was granted.

He organized the band at Fort Gibson. I remember it well; his musicians were nearly all amateurs, and it was some time before his music sounded much better than the howl of a pack of wolves. One day the colonel said to him, "How does your band get along?" "Oh," said he, "dey play hell mit de Chief, and blixon mit Hail Columbia." But the officers had a chance to do better and they determined to get rid of him.

One morning after guard mount the adjutant came to him and asked, "Mr. Hess, what was that last piece of music you played?" The old man expected a compliment, and vigorously tapped his snuff box and offered it to the adjutant, and said, "I make him mid out my own head." "Well," replied the adjutant, "Mr. Hess, you go to the quartermaster and get a spade and pickaxe, and take your music, and go out behind the hospital and dig a deep hole and bury it." The old gentleman was taken by surprise and fell into a very wrathy mood and demanded his discharge at once. The adjutant told him to go down to headquarters and get his discharge; it was all ready for him. "O!" said he, "I will go and I will go right down mit the river." Poor old man, that was the

last I ever saw of him. It was rather a questionable
way of dealing with him. But our band was much
improved by the new band leader, Mr. Walters. But
he did not stay with us long, for he died of fever at
Panama when on our way to California.

My father fought in the war of 1812, and Sackett's
Harbor was familiar ground to him, and on that account the place was of great interest to me. It was
now time for us to leave Sackett's Harbor, and so we
broke camp and started on our way

TO CALIFORNIA.

We first went to Governor's Island, and stayed a
few days, and on the fifth of July, 1852, six of our
companies got on board the splendid steamer Ohio.
We went by the way of Panama, but the other four
companies went by the way of Cape Horn, and did
not reach their destination for about six months after.
After eleven days out we landed at Aspinwall, on the
Isthmus of Panama. We took cars here, eighteen
miles to the Shegress River, when the troops crossed
over to a small place called Georgonia, and marched
to Panama on the Pacific side. The officers' wives
and band, in charge of the quartermaster, Captain

Grant, took small boats and went down the river as far as Cruzes. Here we stayed for the night, and during the night some of the men were taken with the cholera, and the next morning the quartermaster came to me and said, "The government allows twenty dollars to each lady to pay for a mule to cross the isthmus with." And he gave me a twenty-dollar gold piece and told me to go and get a mule for my wife to ride, for Panama was twenty-eight miles away. But the mules were all taken up by other passengers before I got around. I reported to Captain Grant, and he said, then you will have to walk, because the cholera is here, and it is dangerous to remain. Said he, "Your wife cannot go in skirts, you will have to rig her out in male attire; you can use the twenty dollars as you see fit. But drink as little water as possible. You had better get some wine and use instead of water." I told the captain I had a pair of pants my wife could wear, but no coat. Said he, "I have a coat;" and he got one of his own coats, and a cap for her to wear. The pants, of course, were too long, and were rolled up to her knees, and she made such a pretty boy that she attracted the attention of every one, and it amuses me to this day to look back on that picture of forty-seven years ago, and see myself, a young robust man, and my wife in her white pants and white shirt, blue coat and cap trudging beside me, and to add to her peculiar boyish appearance she wore my sash and sword, and carried a haversack with our edibles, and two bottles of claret wine, for which I paid two dollars.

The Spanish residents would say, when seeing the seemingly pretty boy, "Ista boneto machata." A handsome boy. But upon seeing her earrings they would exclaim, "No machata, ista boneto signoreta." Not a boy, but a handsome young girl.

I was afraid my wife could not stand the hardship of the long march; but she stood it well, and it was the very worst time of year to cross the isthmus, for it was in July, the rainy season, and it would come up a rain almost from a clear sky, and pour down in torrents, for five or ten minutes, and then the sun would come out clear and so hot that in a very few minutes it would lick up every bit of moisture, and in a very little while this would be repeated.

The whole way we were passing through forests, which were alive with the chatter of monkeys and song of birds. The monkeys were swinging from branch to branch of the trees and the chatter of the parrots were heard on every hand. One strange scene I remember well. We saw in the ditsance a long green line wriggling along the way; it looked like a mighty serpent, but we soon saw it was too long for a snake and too even in its proportions. Upon nearer inspection we found it was a line of army ants marching and carrying a large green leaf as protection from the sun. At least that seemed to be the purpose from the way each carried the leaf.

The face of the country was mountainous nearly all of the way, and the mountains were very steep, and the roadway a mere path, traversed for ages by pack mules, and they in traversing the mountains had worn stepping stones and even deep holes in the solid rocks. These holes would fill with water, which we found when stepping in were half way to our knees.

We made pretty good progress the first day, and when at night we arrived on top of the mountain we found a rough temporary house on each side of the road. They were mere posts in the ground, the sides bamboo poles endwise, thatched roofs and no floor. We chose the inn called the Elephant on the left side of the road which was about eighty by forty feet in size.

Hammocks were strung around the sides three or four feet apart. I engaged two for our accommodation; then before we retired we went down to a creek and took a bath with our clothes on, for they needed the water as bad as we did. The water was cool and very refreshing, and did us good. When we got back to the house we found several people who had preceded us. Among them a priest and twelve sisters, who were on their way to California. Every one was weary and so retired quite early. As we had no change of clothes we were compelled to sleep in our wet ones. In the night I got cold and thought I would get in the hammock with my wife, and it broke down and the fall hurt me quite severely. In the morning we found the priest had not slept at all; we asked him why, and he said he did not retire because he was afraid if we all slept we would have our throats cut.

In the morning we got some coffee, cold boiled ham and hard bread, also some yams. The yams are similar to our potatoes, though much larger and more mealy and dry. For this I paid one dollar each for the hammocks, and one dollar each for the food. We started on our second day's march down the mountain side, following the mule path, and if we chanced to step in one of the holes the mules had worn in the solid rock we went into the water, often up to the knees, so we were wet all of the time. My wife's feet were blistered, and it was very bad and painful for her the rest of the way. We were also compelled to wade several streams which added to our discomfort. Then on going down the mountain it was very precipitous, and we were compelled to be very careful, for a misstep and a fall were sure death.

As we drew near Panama the road improved, and when we got to the city we were not allowed to carry arms through it, and so I handed my sword to the guard. We were scrutinized very closely, and we had not gone far before we met the American consul, who came galloping up at full speed. He stopped short before us, and said, "When you get into the city do not buy a particle of fruit, for the cholera is raging there, and if you eat fruit you will surely get the cholera. Do not stop, but go right down to the dock, and there is a lighter there which will take you out to the "Golden Gate" (the steamer which was to take us to San Francisco). She lay in the bay about one mile out. As soon as we got in the city we saw some lovely fruit. My wife bought quite a lot to take on the boat. But in a few moments the consul came to us and said, "I told you not to get any fruit; now see what you have done." My wife spoke up and said, "I paid my own money for it." The consul was astonished and replied saying, "I beg your pardon, madam; I thought you were a boy. But you cannot take the fruit on the boat; you may, however, keep the oranges and take the juice on rising in the morning, but the rest of the fruit return and get your money back; then go right down and get aboard the lighter and get on board the ship as soon as possible, where you will be safer from the cholera."

We soon went to the lighter, and as the soldiers had come up, there were fifteen or twenty with us. When we got aboard the ship the mate came and helped each one up, and upon seeing my wife exclaimed, "Do you belong with the troops?" She made no reply, and he repeated his question three times. Then she said, "I am the drum major's wife." "Oh!" said he, "I beg your pardon; I thought you were a boy."

After my wife's heroic feat of making such a long march, she was looked upon with great admiration.

Cholera broke out on shipboard and we lost a good many men, among them Captain Goar. He was a very brave and fine man, loved and mourned by all who knew him.

The cholera was of a very malignant type, and very quick in its action. I have seen men arise from the table after a good dinner and say, "I never felt better in my life," and almost instantly be taken with cramps and die in a few moments. I have seen six or eight bodies lying side by side ready to be disposed of. They were of course thrown into the sea, and it seemed terrible to think perhaps you might be the next to become food for the fishes; and the situation was made more terrible for me as I might have to consign my wife to such a fate or suffer it myself and leave her alone.

The sea burial was performed in this way: There was a weight tied to the feet and a sack sewed around the corpse and it placed upon a plank, one end of which was pushed over the bulwarks, and the other end elevated until the corpse slid into the sea. When the ship is moving the engines cease moving, the bell tolls until the last body disappears; then the ship moves on again.

There were so many sick on shipboard, the doctor ordered the troops put on shore on an island called Tomingo; our tents and the loose baggage was thrown overboard at the same time. After they got on land there were no more cases of cholera, but the troops were dieted on boiled rice or rice soup and coffee. They made no complaint, as they knew it was best. The officers remained on shipboard, and after a stop of two weeks we resumed our course. ·

While my wife and I did not stay on the island, we went ashore to look around, and we gathered some of the most beautiful sea shells I ever saw. We brought a great many with us when we came home. It was here in the Bay of Panama that I first saw a whale. It was a great pleasure to watch them, in schools, sporting and playing like a lot of children. They were not very large; from fifteen to twenty feet long, but large enough to throw water full twenty feet in the air when spouting.

Before we got on shore we lost two of our band, Mr. Herman and George Rogers, the drummer. Mr. Rogers was taken sick early in the morning, and the doctor, worn out, was not up yet, and I did not want to wake him, but after doing all we could for Mr. Rogers we saw we must call the doctor. But it was no use, the poor fellow passed away in one hour.

This was on the 15th of August, 1852.

As soon as the cholera had been stamped out and the ship cleaned, we started on our way again, and there were many amusing scenes on shipboard, of which I will narrate one of them. Every morning the ship had to be cleaned, and through this operation the troops were ordered kept below and a guard stationed at the gangways, with strict orders to let no one pass either way, up or down.

Some men when on guard love to show their authority, and such men will be given all of the opportunity they desire. Sometimes a person who knew nothing of the orders would try to go on deck when he would be stopped and a conversation something like this would take place: "Halt, you can't come up here." "But I must, I have left." "I tell you you can't come up here." "But I want to get a drink of water." "I don't care what you want, I say." "But I will come up," with some vexation. "Get down, I say, Michael, or I will prod you with my bayonet."

This settled it, for of course no one wanted two or three inches of cold steel shoved under his skin. But others would be amused at the earnestness of the guard in showing his authority, and would repeat the attempt to get up stairs, to give the poor fellow a chance to show his authority, as the Irishman said when his wife whipped him, and he went out and whipped his pig, and when asked why he did it said, "It is to show me authority."

The first place we stopped at was Acapulaco, a place in Mexico on the Pacific Ocean, about half way between Panama and San Francisco; it is nearly under the equator, and of course very warm. I have been there twice, and each time the thermometer registered one hundred and fifteen to one hundred and twenty degrees in the shade. The natives take to the water like ducks and hundreds of both sexes may be seen in bathing together, and their bathing suits was only that which nature gave them. But such swimmers the people of the northern clime never saw. The people would throw bright coins into the water to see the natives dive for them. They would get the coin before it had gone three feet under water.

At these places the ship would take on cattle, sheep, hogs, chickens and coal. The natives would bring the coal in sacks, on their heads, from scows anchored alongside the ship. The way cattle and live stock was brought on board was by placing a sling or flat straps around the body of the animal and hoisting them with tackle, by hand or steam. This is cruel; it sometimes drives the breath out of an animal, and then it is quite a task to bring them to. Often the horns of the cattle are knocked off, and the whole process seems a barbarous, cruel method of handling the poor creatures.

We also took on a good deal of fruit at Acapulaco, and it was the finest fruit I ever saw. The pineapples were immense in size, from five to six pounds each; they were so sweet and juicy they would seem to melt in your month.

The next place we stopped was at Santiago, and then we continued on our course to San Francisco. I will never forget

AN AMUSING STORY

I heard on board the boat. I do not know how true it was, but it was told as a truth. Of course, to while the tedious hours while on voyage like this, many funny stories are told, and as ours was a military party the stories told were often concerning the experience of military or naval officers.

Lieut. L. related a story of the experience of one of his classmates of West Point.

It is a well known fact that the boys of West Point as well as college students love to perpetrate practical jokes. This friend of Lieut. L. became a middy on board of one of Uncle Sam's gunboats. I don't remember the name; but one day there came a gawky looking fellow assigned to his ship. This fellow began asking all manner of questions, and the middy determined to perpetrate a joke on him that would put a stop to it. So he said to the gawky, "You are evidently not aware we are all Masons on board this boat, and if you are not a Mason it will be very unpleasant for you." The young man became very anxious and asked the middy how it was possible for him to become a Mason. "Now," said the middy, "I will give you the signs; no one will know but what you are a Mason of long standing." "You should ask all questions of the captain. The next time you wish to know anything go to the captain and ask him, and when he answers you give him the first sign of Masonry by placing the thumb of your left hand to your nose, with the fingers spread apart, the little finger upward. The captain may seem to be very angry, but do not mind that; he is trying you to see if you are a good Mason; so you may then put the thumb of your right hnad to the little finger of the left hand, with the fingers extended at the same angle. He will now seem very angry and order you in irons and put you in the black hole. Never mind that; give him the third sign which is to place your fingers to the corners of your mouth and stretch it as wide as possible. After he has taken you from the black hole he will be your best friend."

This ridiculous performance was gone through with to the letter, and after the poor fellow had suffered in the black hole a couple of days the middy went to the captain and told his story, and stated he was to blame, and what he did it for. Said the captain, "Never do such a thing on board my ship again."

But he ordered the poor fellow released, and it actually did seemingly bring a more kindly feeling and condescension all around.

We got to San Francisco the last of August, 1852, but did not land, but remained in the bay a day, and then went to Benicia, a few miles from there, where we went on shore, and pitched a new lot of tents the government had furnished us for the ones we threw overboard. This was a lovely place for a camp, and was elevated on a high hill in a field of wild oats. But unfortunatly the place, as is nearly all California, was alive with flees. We were supplied with a quantity of Russian insect powder, which seemed to stupify the fleas and we could get some sleep. We were compelled to subsist on government rations, largely, as everything was so very high. Even potatoes were eighteen cents a pound, onions seventeen cents, butter one dollar a pound, and eggs one dollar per dozen, and everything else in proportion. Both male and female help was very high; a man could get five dollars per day doing any kind of work. The price of laundry work was three dollars per dozen. I once saw a washwoman at Benicia who had made sixty thousand dollars washing.

Our six companies stayed here but a few weeks, and then took ship for Fort Vancouver, Washington Territory. We arrived there in September, and two companies with the band relieved the First Artillery. The quarters were built of logs, but were very comfortable. My quarters were in the rear of the band room, and was covered with heavy canvas and was fixed up very nicely.

A short time after we came here I became

A STOCK RAISER.

For this I must thank the late General Grant. As I have said, he was our quartermaster, and was raising stock himself. He came to me one day and said, "I have a fine sow about to give birth to a litter of pigs; you have a great deal of slops from the band mess room, and instead of throwing it away to rot and create disease, feed it to the sow and you may have the pigs." I thanked him and took the sow under my care, and soon had as fine a lot of little pigs as a stock raiser could wish for. All did well, and in a short time I sold those pigs to a farmer, near, for the enormous sum of forty dollars apiece. This was the first money I saved from fifteen years of government service. Thanks to my old friend, Captain Grant.

The farmer who bought the pigs had been a soldier; his name was Kane; his time of service having expired, he was sharp enough to see what could be done there at farming and stock raising and so engaged in it.

Captain Grant was a frequent visitor at my quarters. Nearly every day he went his rounds of inspection, and would ride up and knock at the door with his riding whip and pass the time of day, and then dash away at full speed.

AN OCCASIONAL EPISODE

of army life in those days, was not unlike some of those of the present time, though not to be commended, but rather to show how foolish man can be, I will relate a little incident of our army life at this post.

When the troops we relieved were about to depart, the officers gave a reception, and as is usual on such occasions tobacco and wine circulated pretty freely.

On this occasion everybody got full, I with the rest. The whole band included. As would naturally be the case, conversation drifted to the merits of the armies of the world. We had in the band an Englishman, a very good-natured fellow by the name of Young, and as would be perfectly natural, Mr. Young defended the merits of the English Army. But I could not stand it to hear a man in the pay of Uncle Sam talk in favor of the army of another country, and I lost my head, that is, what was not already lost in a muddled state on account of the liquor. I insisted he should take it back or go and fight it out. But he declined to do either, as I was an officer and could have him arrested for striking an officer, but I told him I would lay rank aside. He finally consented, and after showing me he could handle me helped me home, and of course we were just as good friends after the liquor was gone as before. But it goes to show that by force of circumstances it comes as easy, once in a, while, for a soldier to raise h—l as it is to raise pigs.

While we were here we built a theater. As before stated, we had excellent dramatic talent, and while here we formed a Thespian society, of which I and my wife were members. Our troop did not confine themselves to dramas and farces alone, but played a number of Shakesperian pieces, such as Hamlet, Richard the Third, Macbeth, Othello and others; also Douglass, The War Lock of the Glen, Lady of Lyons, Golden Farmer, Robert McCair and many others.

HOW I BECAME A CIRCUS MAN.

While here I got a furlough for myself and four of the band to go out with a circus, through a part of Oregon. The owner's name was Cadwell. I was to receive ten dollars per day and each of the men five dollars per day and expenses. It was a pretty good outfit, but destined to misfortune.

There is a man in Detroit, a well known musician here, whose name is Frees. Mr. Frees was a member of the band, and requested to be one of the number. He said he did not care so much for the money as to see the country. Well, we will hear from Mr. Frees about the country as we go further on.

We first went to Portland, Oregon. It was at this time a very small place of not more than five hundred inhabitants. Before reaching Portland we had to cross the Columbia River. This river is over a mile in width, and the water is deep enough for large steamers, and the river was alive with salmon.

After crossing the river we traveled a strip of land three miles wide, and then reached the Willamette River, not as large a stream as the Columbia River. On the opposite side of this river stands Portland. At this point the two streams form an isthmus, but increases in width below.

We made our first stand in Portland, and went from there to Oregon City. From Oregon City the band and clown took a small steamer to a little town we nicknamed Graball, because of the high prices charged for everything. I do not remember its real name. The boat we were on was called the Sholewater. This was its first trip. We had gone but a few miles when the boiler head blew off and the hot steam and mud flew in every direction. The band was playing on deck at the time. But the steam blew so much harder than we did, the music stopped very quick. Mr. Frees threw down his instrument, and crying, "My poor wife, what will she do?" and was about to spring overboard when I caught him; otherwise he would have found a watery grave.

No one was hurt by the explosion, but quite a number were thrown into the water. One of the people
blown into the water was a Hebrew, who had his wife
and children with him, and his first words after being
fished out of the water, was not to inquire for his wife
and children, but was, "Oh! mine Got, mine Got, my
hundred and fifty tolar gold watch ish ruined, it ish
spoilt."

Well, we had a time before we got to town. We
were billed to play that night, and had ten miles to
walk over the worst road you ever saw. We followed
a road which took us away from the river. But the
pesky road run out, and I had to guide my party by
instinct, for I had no other means. But again we
came to the river, and I saw a boat on the other side,
and signaled to the boatman, who took us over. We
finally arrived, but too late, and did not play that
night. But the next day and night we played to good
houses. But a very funny episode took place here.
Of course the country was new and everything scarce,
and the hotels were of a very crude order.

The professional name of our clown was Mariman.
Whether it was his real name or not I do not know.
But in the morning the landlord startled everybody

by calling loudly, "Mr. Mariman, Mr. Mariman, get up, please; I want your sheet for a tablecloth." We had to walk most of the time when going from place to place, because the roads were so bad. There is so much rain in this country that the people of California declared that Oregon people were web footed. At any rate, the country was flooded, and the sun dried a crust very quickly, and you would step on apparently dry ground, only to break through into deep mud and water. This kept Mr. Frees continually damning the country, and I would retort by saying, "Mr. Frees, I thought you wished to see the country."

This would bring a look from him of horror, disgust and anger. These terrible roads caused many delays, and also prevented the people from coming long distances to see the show, and for this reason the circus was compelled to break up. Had the manager waited until after the wet season was over it would have been a great success. We stopped upon the open prairie, on high ground, not a building in sight, and yet the people came from all directions and filled our tent to its greatest capacity. We stopped at every town until we reached Marysville, when we started on our return trip to Fort Vancouver, and right glad we were to get there.

I LEAVE THE UNITED STATES ARMY.

The following December, 1853, I received my discharge, dated from January 16th, 1854, the date of expiration of fifteen years continuous service in the United States Army. This was the hardest trial to me I had ever been called upon to endure. The army had been my home so long, it was like tearing out my very heart strings to leave it. But for my wife's sake I must leave. She had left her mother at the age of sixteen, and she was anxious to get back to see her, and of course it was a pleasure to grant her that privilege. But I must go somewhere to make some money to get home with and have enough left to do business with.

Our leave taking with our friends in the army was an affecting scene. Both officers and men vied with each other in their attempts to do us honor and make the occasion as pleasant as possible.

The adjutant is the secretary of a regiment, and all orders or sentiment of the colonel and regiment are expressed through him, and here are the sentiments, still legible, though faint, on the letter I received from the adjutant:

"Headquarters Fourth United States Infantry, Adjutant's Office, Fort Vancouver, W. T., Dec. 27th, 1853.—Sergeant, as you are about to receive your discharge from the United States service, I take pleasure in testifying to the very commendable and praiseworthy manner in which you have conducted yourself during the time you have been connected with the Fourth Infantry. During the seven years I have known you, I have found you always attentive to your duties, and as a soldier you enjoy the confidence of every officer with whom you have served, and your meritorious conduct in the battles of Mexico will not seen be forgotten by them. Should you commence business in civil life I offer you my best wishes for your success, and should you feel inclined to enter again in the military service I can assure you that the officers of the regiment will take pleasure in having you appointed to the post in non-commissioned staff which you now occupy. Very respectfully, Thos. R. McConnell, Adjutant."

On the 28th of December my wife and I took a small boat and went down the Columbia River to the mouth of the Willamette River, and thence to Portland, where we took the steamer Fremont for San Francisco. After a rough passage we were landed at the dock of the Golden City. We registered at the Crescent City Hotel. It seemed very strange to pay for all we got, after being with Uncle Sam so long and having everything furnished for us. I had to pay thirty-two dollars a week for board. It was pretty high, but some places board was much higher. The first job I got was on the 22d of February. I played for the Shields Guard, a cavalry company. I had a horse and uniform furnished me, and twenty-five dollars for one hour. After that I joined the American Brass Band. I did very well at this for some time, but I left the hotel and rented rooms. After this I opened a cigar store on Montgomery street. I paid $75 a month for a small space in a restaurant. The place I occupied was eight feet by six. I did well here until I got something better. At this time lottery and gambling was allowed. A company by the name of Smith, Gaylord & Co. had gotten up a lottery for $100,000; $10,000 in gold as the chief prize.

Mr. Gaylord came to see me and he wanted me to sell
tickets for him. He told me I could make more in
one day selling tickets than I could make in a week
selling cigars. He said I could rent a room, and he
would allow me a commission of twenty-five per cent.
He gave me a gold watch as a sample. There were
two hundred of them, and he would allow me a commission of twenty-five per cent, so I accepted his
offer and sold out my stock of tobacco and got a
store on Kearney street and Commercial street
for five dollars a day. I did the best business at
night. I was green at the business for a few days. I
improved as I went along. I got a boy to ring a bell
for three hours each night, and gave him five dollars
for his services. He would stand in front of the office
and ring the bell to draw the crowd. I never knew
how to make money until I went into business. I
thought it was a bad day if I did not make fifty dollars. Sometimes I would sell four or five hundred
tickets a day. The tickets were one dollar apiece. I
have often disposed of fifty to one man. I would
close up at eleven o'clock at night, and put the money
in my handkerchief and take it home, and we would
count it up, and put the gold in separate piles and

silver dollars, halves and quarters. I would take to the gambling houses in the morning and get one per cent premium for it. You must know there was no paper money in those days, for this was the golden period of California. The first prize, ten thousand dollars, was drawn · by a small boy who took two tickets, one for his sister in New York, and he kept one for himself. The one he had won first prize. He was a poor boy who had worked his passage to California. He was employed in a store as chore boy. The money was deposited in Palmer, Cook & Co.'s bank, and ,it was all in fifty dollar slugs, as we called them. He was given a certificate of deposit by the committee, and they went down with the boy and took it out of the bank. The drawing took place July 4th, 1854. This came on Monday, and the Saturday before I sold eight hundred tickets. All stores and public places were closed on Sunday. On Saturday preceding the drawing a man came to me and gave me his card and asked me to call on him at his store, 151 Commerce street. I told him I would. I called on him Monday morning. He had a large jewelry store, and he had a lottery also. He asked me if I would come to his store and sell tickets for him. I

TAKEN AT SAN FRANCISCO, CAL., 1854 (FROM AN
AMBROTYPE).

told him I would, and he told me he would give me fifteen per cent and I could have a place at his counter. I said that would do, so I went at it. There were three others beside myself selling tickets. But I sold more than all the rest together. My employer's name was Robert Mayers. He was an Englishman, and as nice a man as I have ever met. He wanted me to come and live in one of his houses, of which he had six on Stockton and Lombard streets.

But soon after this the State put a stop to the lottery business and left me without an occupation, and I joined a band and we got an engagement to play on a steamboat called Defender, Captain Brown, of New York. She was running in opposition to the old Combine. She ran from San Francisco to Sacramento. We would leave San Francisco in the afternoon at five o'clock and get to Sacramento in the morning. The old line charged ten dollars each way. Our boat charged firty cents. This caused much bitterness, and they would fire at us every time we would come together, but no one was hurt. After a while the boat went on the drydock, and my occupation was gone so far as the boat was concerned.

After this my wife and I took the road with the Ferry Minstrels, a good company. We gave entertainments in all of the principal towns in the state. We crossed the Sierra Nevada Mountains on horseback; the distance from Chasta to Weaverville is forty miles; we made it in one day, and played that night. It must have been hard for the girls who had to dance, for it made me so lame I did not get over it for some time. A young lady by the name of Carrie Finn, who was a member of the troop, was riding in company with my wife, and as they were going down the mountain, it was pretty steep, and just at the foot of the mountain was a small stream of water, and they were going very fast; as Miss Finn's horse came to the water it stopped so sudden it sent her on the other side. She left her seat as nice as you please, and sat down on the opposite bank and without injury.

HOW I BECAME A GOLD MINER.

We arrived at Weaverville about five o'clock in the afternoon, and Sunday morning I took a stroll around to see some of the mines. It being Sunday all the mines were closed. I came to a place where they had been digging for gold. I could get no spade, as they were all packed away, so I went to dig with my hand. I did not work but a moment till I felt something hard; this was in the sand. When I came to examine what it was I found I had dug a piece of pure gold; the piece was quite small, but now I could say I had dug gold.

I went through thirty or forty mining towns while I was traveling with the troop; gold was plenty at this time. When coin was not obtainable the landlords would take a pinch of gold dust, with the thumb and first finger, for a drink. A person with a large hand could take dust enough to make a ten dollar piece. Most everybody had nuggets or dust. People were known to have gone in the mountains and in crevices of the rocks cut large nuggets out, some of which would be worth hundreds and some thousands of dollars.

California is a lovely country, but subject to earthquakes, and I think in time San Francisco will go down. It has all the appearance of it. The Bay of San Francisco was formed by some volcanic eruption. To just look at the high hills and immense quantity of rocks thrown up hundreds of feet, all go to show what nature has done to bring it about.

After my season expired with this troop we returned to our old home on Stockton street, where we stayed until we got ready to go east.

It was customary when the mail steamer comes through the Golden Gate to fire a cannon as a signal that the mail is coming. Immediately after this there is a rush for the postoffice. I have been in line in single file when the line would extend all of two blocks. We would only get news once in two weeks, and I tell you it would make a man feel good to get a letter from the east.

One morning about three o'clock we were wakened by a terrible noise, as loud as a hundred cannon at once; just before that we experienced a great shake up. It nearly shook us out of bed. All of the bells rang, the clocks stopped, and there was a general shaking up. My wife did not know what it was, but I did, but did not tell her so. The next morning she read an account of a great earthquake that did much damage. At one of the hotels, the Rezet House, men were seen coming out of rooms not their own and women the same, so excited was everybody. The

Rezet House at that time was seven stories high, and of course got the heaviest shaking up. It frightened my wife very much; she had seen death on every hand, where they were dying with cholera, and it did not frighten her. But the earthquake was too much for her. She was now more anxious to see her mother than ever.

TERRIBLE TIMES IN CALIFORNIA.

At this time no person was safe on the street; there were so many murders committed every day, and if the man who committed it had money he would get off. One night General Richardson, United States Marshal, and his wife were at the Metropolitan Theater, and a man by the name of Charles Corry was sitting immediately in front of the marshal; he kept looking over at a woman in the rear of the general, a woman of bad repute, and an associate of Corry's; she kept up the flirtation with Corry all the time, but Gen. Richardson did not look back, and he supposed Corry was laughing at his wife. After the first act they both went in the hall; they had some words, and the general pulled Corry's nose, but Gen. Richardson's friends separated them.

The next night they met on some street and Corry took the General by his arm as if to apologize, and when he got him where he wanted him he stabbed him to the heart. Richardson died in a few moments. But not until he had told who killed him. Corry was arrested and imprisoned, but the woman said she had sixty thousand dollars to spend in his defence and this in such a place would free him. The next day another murder took place in the day time. James King, of William, the editor of an evening paper called the "Evening Bulletin;" he had said something in his paper the evening before that reflected on the character of a man by the name of James P. Casey, who was also an editor of a small paper, and as James King, of Williams, was crossing the street, Casey met him and shot him dead. The editor James King, of Williams, was well liked by all good citizens, as he was doing all he could for reform. There were so many murders and crimes took place no one was safe, especially if it was known a person had money. One day I thought I would put my money in the bank. I had one thousand dollars, and I deposited it in Palmer

& Co.'s bank. But a few days after they closed their
doors. But three weeks after they opened again and
I got my money out again. After that I was at a loss
to know what to do with it. We had a bag of potatoes
in the kitchen, and I thought this would be a very
good place to hide my gold. In a few days my wife
was cleaning house and emptied the contents of the
bag out on the commons, near the house, and thought
no more about it until night; then it came to her mind
that she had thrown the money out with the contents
of the sack of potatoes. The money consisted of fifty-
dollar gold pieces; they were put in a buckskin bag
just large enough to put one on each other, as close
as they could be stowed away. As soon as she discovered her loss she told Mrs. Caleb, a lady who we were
staying with, what she had done. Mrs. Caleb told her
to go and look for it. She said "no, it is gone, I saw
some rag-pickers with their sticks taking the rags out,
and they have taken it away." "Well," said she, "if
you don't go and look for it, I will." She did go and
found it. Wasn't my wife glad. "Now," said she to
my wife, "don't tell your husband about it; if you do
he will be telling you about it all the time." She
never mentioned it until we came to Detroit the sec-

ond time in 1857. We were talking together one night when she told me the story.

At the time of this great epidemic of crime in California, the best citizens formed a vigilant committee to subdue the tough element, who were a lot of cutthroats and robbers.

In a few days they had eight thousand men enrolled, a great many of whom had been in the army. Besides the military companies the firemen in the city joined the vigilants. They were well armed and meant business.

They formed on Montgomery street and went to the jail; they surrounded the jail, having two batteries of artillery with pieces all loaded with ball; they then demanded the two prisoners, James P. Casey and Charles Corry, the two murderers of James King, of William, and the United States Marshall, Gen. Richardson; the officials of the jail delivered them to the committee without any resistance; they were taken away in a close carriage.

They were tried at once and sentenced to be hung. The signal was to hang them when the funeral procession passed Commercial and Kerney streets. I was playing in the procession that day, and when

we got to Commercial street we looked down and
we could see them suspended from the windows of
the fort. After this I saw Hetrington and Brace hung
by the same body of men. There were fifty men,
composed of some of the most respectable citizens of
the city, who were chosen as executive committee. If
they wanted any person they would give the order
for their arrest, and it would be done, and when the
bell rang, that was the signal for them to assemble.
This made the evildoers tremble whenever that bell
rang. But only murderers were hung; other criminals
were sent out of the city. They sent some to New
York and others out of the country; they took the
sheriff of the county, and sent him together with several more of the same sort out of the city.

The sheriff's name was Scanlen. Jim Turner and
Charlie Duan, chief of the fire department, and Yankee Sullivan, the pugilist. They put Sullivan in Fort
Vigilance, and he cut one of his veins in his arm and
bled to death. After this everything was quiet. If
there were any other bad characters, they kept quiet.

WE LEAVE CALIFORNIA.

It was now getting late in the fall and my wife was getting very anxious to see home. We took the next steamer and started for Panama. We had Christmas on the Pacific Ocean and New Year's on the Atlantic Ocean.

When we got to Panama, we did not walk this time; they had finished the railroad to Aspinwall, on the Atlantic side. At Aspinwall we found the steamer George Law ready to sail the next day. So we went on board of her and started for New York. It was very rough on the Gulf of Tewantepic, but we arrived in New York at night. The very next trip the George Law made she went down in a gale. All of her passengers and crew, consisting of seven hundred and fifty souls, went down on her, not one of whom were saved.

We stayed in New York a few days, and went to Syracuse, where I had a relation. We stopped with one of my brothers' who kept the Salt Springs Hotel, for two weeks after. Then we came to Detroit for the second time, where I have been ever since.

I BECAME A MEMBER OF THE DETROIT LIGHT GUARDS.

Shortly after coming to Detroit I turned out with the Detroit Light Guard on the Fourth of July as drum major, in 1857. A few days after this I joined that organization, and was with them as musician and armorer for thirty-three years, and am now a veteran member of that corps. Some of the most pleasant times I ever had were with the Detroit Light Guards. At that time the company got nothing from the State. They had to pay for all they got; uniforms and all would have to be paid for by the company. I found the men to be all gentlemen of wealth and prominence, who had joined the company just for the pleasure they would derive by being a soldier, and they all proved worthy the name. I will name a few of the most prominent men who were in the company at that time: Gen. A. S. Williams, Capt. T. W. Palmer, Alfred Russell, C. A. T. Trowbridge, E. D. Trowbridge, Oliver Goldsmith, Merick Penny, G. W. Thayer, Jerome Croul, James Pittman, Mart Smith, W. D. Wilkins and W. C. Mabury. I only mention some of the most wealthy and influential men just to show what class of men the Detroit Light Guards were composed of. Most all of the men had shields with their number, in gold or silver, put on the stock of their muskets. They were owned by the company, and not the State. I knew every number so well that I could pick a man's gun out of the rack in the dark. The stocks were varnished, the locks and screws blued, with burnished barrels. I did it all myself. After the first battle of Bull Run they were turned over to the Ordnance Department at Washington, with a lot of tents the company had of their own.

The first time I went with the Detroit Light Guard was in November, 1857, when they went to Milwaukee to visit the Light Guard of that city. We had a good time and they gave us a fine reception and a ball. They took the Light Guard Band with them, and I was the drum major. We went by boat from Grand Haven, and the company met us at the dock and took us up to the city. The next day it snowed all day, but we marched through slush and mud all over the city. Gen. A. S. Williams was Captain of the company then, and James Pittman was First Lieutenant. We had a good band. Henry Kern was the leader, and we were highly complimented for our fine music. We left there on the 14th of November on our return trip. It was blowing a perfect hurri-

cane when we left Milwaukee, and the boat we went
aboard of was an old tub of a thing— a side-wheeler.
It put one in mind of some of the boats on the Ohio
River. It was very rough when we got out. I didn't
think we would ever see Detroit again. John Merrill
got very frightened, and he went up to the captain at
the pilot house, scudding under bare poles, with his
big bear skin shako on his head, and prayed the captain to return. But he could not prevail on him to
return. The captain told him that his boat never
went back. It was amusing to see Johnny in such a
rig on such a cold night. When we got to Grand
Haven, the next morning, the ice was so thick that
we had a hard time to get to the dock. We got on
the cars about 8 o'clock, and stopped at Grand Rap-
ids and stayed over night and came home the next
morning. When we got to the depot, Gen. Williams
turned the command of the company over to Lieut.
Pittman and took a hack to his home. After we went
to the armory—it was Sunday, and the anniversary of
the organization—we were marched to our quarters.
Lieut. Pittman said a few words to the men, and then
said: "I propose three silent cheers for wives and
sweethearts," and they were given in a low breath. I
went with the company wherever they went, and attended all the encampments with them. I remember

when we went to Whitmore Lake, a few miles from
Ann Arbor. We boarded at a hotel. One day at
dinner the waiters cme around to the men and told
them what kind of a desert they had. They said ap-
ple pie, mince pie, huckleberry pie, and the like. Mr.
Kern, one of the band, said he would take "hookleboy" pie. You should have heard the roar that went
up from the boys—"Hookleboy," "Hookleboy pie"—
they had it all over the camp. The last word at night
and the first word spoken in the morning was "hookleboy, hookleboy." Mr. Kern said to me, "Mr. Elderkin, if they don't stop saying 'hookleboy' to me, I will
take my instrument and go home." Now, almost
every person knew Mr. Kern. He was a large man,
weighing three hundred and seventy-five pounds, a
good, honest, outspoken man, and a fine musician.
He is the one President Lincoln said "was
the biggest blower in the service." I told
the men how sensitive he was, and told them to
be a little careful and not plague him so much. For
a time it was stopped, and then broke out again as bad
as ever. Then something new came up to attract
their attention.

Corporal Brenan got on a bender, and when we were all in camp there he took off all of his clothes but his shirt, and got on a horse and rode it all over the town, and up to the hotel. The guard was sent for and he was put in the guard house. He declared he was "Mazeppa."

When I first joined the company the armory stood where Edson & Moore's store now stands, and where the old Post and Tribune building stood. Dr. Schofield had his office in the building.

After I became leader of the Detroit Light Guard Band we played once a week at West Grand Circus Park, and the citizens living convenient to the park clubbed in and paid us for our services. Gov. Bagley would send out the cigars and lemonade to us whenever we played. Large crowds would be there at every concert. Little Fred Eberts, a little tot about eight years old, son of Comrade F. H. Eberts of this city, would always be there. He was quite a musician himself. He would go on the stand and I would let him take the drum and play a selection with us. He would want me to play "Sally Waters." It seemed to be his favorite, for he would ask for it. But I did not have that piece, so he would say, "Well, play

'Yankee Doodle.'" That was the next to "Sally Waters" for him. He would come down to the armory
almost every day and try to find a cap or coat that
would fit him. There was at that time a suit of
clothes made for Larnard Williams, son of the late
Gen. Williams. Larney was a marker. He had out-
grown the uniform, and of course it was no use to
anyone. Fred was there one day and I showed it to
him and told him he could have it. He was tickled
almost to death. He took his uniform home, and Mrs.
Eberts put it away. Fred, his father, had got himself
a new suit, also blue, which he paid fifty dollars for.
Mrs. Eberts, the boy's mother, was out one day, and
the youngster thought he would make some altera-
tion in his suit. So he went to the wardrobe, and, as
he supposed, got his suit out. He took a pair of
shears and cut off the legs of the pants and cut off the
sleeves of the coat. His mother came home before
he had finished his job. As quick as she saw what he
had done, she threw up her hands and cried out:
"Why, Freddie Eberts, what have you done? You
have ruined your father's new suit!" He had mis-
taken his father's new suit for his own.

I ENLIST FOR MY THIRD WAR.

I had passed through the Florida, or Seminole war, and the Mexican war without receiving serious injuries, though I still carry a piece of lead in the calf of my leg received at Matamoras, Mexico. But this did not dampen my military ardor. So when the great Rebellion of 1861 took place, I determined to go if the Detroit Light Guard went. That company became the first company, or Company A, of the First Michigan Infantry. I enlisted for three months' service. We were stationed at Fort Wayne until the 13th day of May, 1861. The regiment started for Washington, and I with them as drum major of that regiment. We got on board the old propeller Missouri, and went to Cleveland. From there we took cars by way of Pittsburg to Washington, where we arrived in due time.

While in Washington we were complimented as having the best band in the city, considering the number of pieces. On Saturday evening the staff and company officers, with a number of citizens of Michigan who were temporarily sojourning there, called

upon the President, with the band of the regiment,
and honored him with a serenade. The President appeared in response and was loudly cheered. He made
a few complimentary remarks, declining to make a
speech, and invited the company into the famous East
Room, where Colonel Wilcox was foramlly presented
by Adjutant-General Thomas, and afterwards each of
the officers and citizens by the Colonel. The President then expressed a desire that the band should be
presented. Then I was first introduced, and afterwards Mr. Henry Kern, the leader, and the privates.
The President had a word of welcome for each, and
a supply of compliments for me, whose previous services had been mentioned to him, and for Mr. Kern,
whom he facetiously styled the "biggest blower" in
the service, as Mr. Kern weighed 375 pounds. Both
the President and General Thomas spoke in the high-
est terms of our music, and notified me that during our
stay in Washington we would be expected to alternate
with Sousa's Marine Band and with the Rhode Island
band in furnishing music for the afternoon concerts
which were given three times a week in the grounds
back of the presidential mansion. This compliment
had great meaning, when it is stated that such a re-

quest had not been made of Dodsworth's band, which accompanied the Twelfth New York Regiment, nor of any of the Seventh Regiment band, nor of any of the other equally famous bands that numbered two or three times the pieces of our favorite Light Guard band.

On turning from the band, the President excused his ignorance of military etiquette, and requested Gen. Thomas to address his visitors. The General very briefly alluded to the impression the regiment had created in military circles, repeating some of the compliments that had previously been paid them, and promised them every consideration and service it would be in his power to grant them. The President advanced and shook hands with Col. Wilcox, asking at the same time if he was comfortably quartered. The Colonel replied that if he was to change at all he should merely desire to camp on the opposite side of the river. The President laughed, and said that the permission would be given in a few days. He then retired and the company withdrew. The band played the National airs and "Marseilles" on the outside, after which cheers were given for the President and the serenade was concluded. Gen. Thomas then escorted the party to the residence of the Secretary of War. Here, too, the company was invited in and were severally presented and received a surfeit of compliments. They next called on Gen. Scott. The old veteran sent an aidecamp to express his regrets that he was so indisposed as to be unable to receive the entire party, and to invite in Col. Wilcox. Col. Wilcox, accompanied by Gen. Thomas, went in, and had quite a lengthy interview. The General expressed his greatest satisfaction at the reports which had reached him of the discipline, military accomplishments and gentlemanly bearing of his command, which he hoped soon to have the pleasure of witnessing in person. He promised that at an early day they should have all the active service they might desire. The evening was so far advanced on leaving Gen. Scott's that it was not deemed proper to make any more calls, and the party returned to their quarters in high spirits, after passing a most agreeable evening.

I should have mentioned that while at the White House the President expressed a desire to visit the regimental headquarters and witness a dress parade of the regiment. Of course the Colonel was only too happy of the opportunity of receiving such a distinguished mark of consideration. "The visit will be paid at an early day this week," said the President. The usual course heretofore had been for regiments to call upon the President for review, and frequently it required great influence to induce him to suspend his business to perform that service. In this instance he departs from all established customs and himself seeks the opportunity of conferring this honor. No more signal mark of the position the regiment occupied could be given. One night, a few days after this, Col. Wilcox sent for me, and said he would like me to get a bugle and go with him. We were about to cross the Potomac and go to Alexandria, Virginia. He told me to see the Quartermaster, and he would give me a horse. I was to leave the band in Washington and go with him. I did not like this very much, as I was Drum Major. I thought he ought to take a sergeant for his orderly. I was looking out for a good time. I knew if I went with him I would have lots to do, and that is what I didn't like; but I did not tell him so. I loved the Colonel very much, and he liked me and wanted to put me forward. But I was not ambitious and was contented in the position that I held. The night the army left Washington for

Alexandria, we sat up all night, without a wink of sleep, and commenced to cross the long bridge in the morning. We got there just at break of day. We went right to the depot. As we were passing King street, I looked down the street and saw a steamboat about to land. She had soldiers on board, and Col. Ellsworth, with the Chicago Zouaves, were on board. As soon as they got on shore they marched up King street to the Marshall House. There was a rebel flag on the top of the house, and Col. Ellsworth went to the top of the house to take the flag down. As he was coming down with it, Jackson, the proprietor of the house, fired on him with a shotgun and killed him. The next instant one of Col. Ellsworth's men shot Jackson. That was the first blood shed for the cause of the Union. If we had been five minutes sooner we would have got the train of cars, going to Richmond, as they had just run out. We took the track up for some distance. Here we took Capt. Ball and his company. After this we went on the top of Shuter Hill, a very high place, and pitched our tents.

After we had been here a few days the rebel pickets commenced to annoy us a great deal, and when they would fire on our pickets I would have to saddle my horse and go with the Colonel out to the picket line and see what it was about, and after all was quiet, go back to the camp and wait for a second alarm. Sometimes it would occur two or three times during the night. The rebels would sneak up to our pickets and kill some of them, and then would leave and come back later. This was kept up all the time we were there. After a short time I told Col. Wilcox I would like him to relieve me, as I did not like to take care of a horse and be disturbed so much in the night. The Colonel, at my request, relieved me, and had a sergeant take my place.

We had a good time in camp. Guard mount would take place down town near the postoffice, and most all the city would be there to see the fun and hear the music. I forgot to mention that one day when we were in Washington it was our day to give a concert in the park in the rear of President Lincoln's house. We had played several selections, when I received a card, written in pencil in a very fine hand, requesting us to play a selection from "Ill Trovatore." I gave the card to Mr. Kern, the leader, and they played it very fine. It was a very long selection. It commenced with the Anvil Chorus and ended with

"Missearare, I long to rest me." I never heard it played better in my life. After we finished the piece a man came out of the President's house, with a straw hat and brown linen coat and pants, and said the piece was well executed—remarkably well—and handed me a twenty-dollar gold piece, and told me when we went down to stop at the Kirkwood and treat the band. He said, if I liked, I could get in his carriage and go with him. I excused myself and told him I would go with the band. He said he had loaned the United States one million dollars, and he would let Uncle Sam have another million if they stood in need of it. He was a fine-looking man, large and splendid form. By looking at him closely I could see he was of Indian extraction. I think he was a Cherokee. He said he was an Indian. Said he, "My wife is waiting for the President, and he has gone out." On looking up, he said, "There she comes now," and left me. I never thought to ask him name.

Now I will go back to Alexandria, where we left off at Shuter's Hill. We had a great deal of wildcat money with us, and some plank road paper. It looked nice, and I had quite a lot of it; but I got rid of it all. They were glad to get it.

Comrade Fred Eberts, of the Light Guard, was a good soldier and full of his jokes. I don't know how it was, but he had chickens most all the time. I have often seen him on picket duty, and when he came back to camp he would have five or six chickens hung over his musket. I did not know him as well as I do now. If I had, I might have had some of his goodies. I was down town one day in a saloon—I think there were eight of us in the saloon—when Comrade Fred Eberts came in with a young and pretty lad. As he came in he looked around and saw me. He said, "How are you, Jim? Will you have a glass of soda water?" I said I didn't mind; so he treated all of us, and put his hand in his pocket and fished out a handful of plank road money. He got good money back for change. We thought nothing of that, as most all Michigan men had that kind of money. I did not go with the regiment when they went to Bull Run. I was to have gone with Col. Wilcox, but he forgot to send his orderly to me with his horse. He told me he would, but it slipped his mind, so I stayed with the band at Cloud's mill. I have always been glad I did not go, for if I had I would have had to make good time back to Washington.

After the regiment came back to Washington we went into camp at Arlington Heights and were mustered out of service. But the regiment came back to Detroit without their arms, as they had been turned over to the Ordnance Department for future use. When we got off the cars at the foot of Brush street there was a large crowd there to receive us.

After I came home I went with the Light Guard and remained with them for a short time. Then I recruited a band for the Fifth Infantry and went to Washington, with Lieut. Henry Hodson, and from there to Alexandria, Va., and from there to Camp Michigan, below Alexandria.

The Second, Third and Fifth Michigan, together with the Thirty-seventh New York and the Fire Zouaves, were in our brigade. Col. Terry was in command of the Fifth and Col Poe of the Second. "Old Fighting Dick" Richardson, as we called him, had command of the brigade. Some very amusing scenes occurred at different times while we were here. One day they had brigade drill, and all the rest of the regiments were in their proper place but ours. Col. Terry could not get in line. Gen. Richardson said, "Are you ready?" "No, General, not yet." After a long pause—"Col. Terry," in a little more stern voice, "Are you ready?" "Yes, General, all ready now." "Not by a d—n sight!" replied Gen. Richardson. "Get your men in line." Gen. Richardson was a fine disciplinarian on duty, and as brave as a lion. But off duty he would be seen in linen pants, shirt sleeves and straw hat, and he had many most comical ways.

One day he had been to the city and bought a new hat, and rode through the camp holding on to the horse's mane, and all ran out of their tents to see him. "There goes Fighting Dick," they would say. "Oh, Dick has got a new hat. But everybody loved Gen. Dick. He was promoted to Division General, and he left us. He did not like to leave us. He thought Michigan men were the boys to fight.

One morning, when we were at Williamsburg, he came over to see us before we had had our breakfast. Some were standing around a fire we had made, and he commenced to talk and joke. Said he, "They took me from my old regiment. I would rather have one regiment of Michigan troops than ten thousand other troops."

After passing the winter at Camp Michigan, we got orders to go to Fortress Monroe.

Mr. Stack and I were chums. He was leader of the Third Michigan Band and I was leader of the Fifth Michigan Band. Stack was a German, and a small man, and had a wife of very tall stature. She was Irish, nearly six feet tall, and as straight as a rush. We ranked as second lieutenants. After we got orders to leave Camp Michigan to go to Fortress Monroe, Mrs. Stack and my wife went to Washington and remained there until after I was discharged. They rented rooms there and kept house. Some very funny things occurred when we were at the camp. Mr. Kern, the large man, had a habit of snoring. His tent was next to that of mine, and it made it disagreeable for my wife, whose health was not of the best, and that constant snoring was the means of keeping her awake a great deal. The two drummers, Taglor and Oliver Bloom, occupied the tent with Mr. Kern. They were unable to sleep, and so Mr. Kern said to them, "I will tell you what to do. When I go to bed to-night, you take this string and tie it around my big toe, and when I snore give it a pull, and that will wake me, so you can sleep, and it will perhaps be the means of breaking me of that bad habit of snoring." Well, they went at it the first night. As soon as he

would fall asleep, Bloom would jerk the string and
the snoring would cease; but it would be but momen-
tarily, for the snoring commenced harder than ever.
They told me the next morning that the thing did not
work. You, see, they slept in different beds, Kern
on one side and Taglor and Bloom on the other side
of the tent. Taglor died some years ago and Bloom
is in the postoffice, and has been there since Mr. Swift
took charge of it.

They asked me what I could do about that snoring.
I told them they would get used to it after a while,
and then they would not mind it. My tent was close
to Mr. Harris, the suttler's tent, and the sentinel
walked just in rear of my tent. They would meet
there and talk together. My wife would make coffee
almost every night and take it out to them and they
would drink it on post. This was in the winter
and it was very cold, and three or four inches of snow
on the ground. One night, after we were in bed, the
guard met. They talked of old times and things they
had done before they went in the army. One of them
said to the other, "Bill, I wish I were in Michigan to-
night and had a piece of calico in a cutter. How

happy I would be." A few days after this he went on picket duty and was killed.

As I said before, Mrs. Stack and my wife went to Washington during my absence in the army. I saw my wife on the boat and looked at her until she was out of sight. I cannot express my feelings at parting with my dear wife at that time—one who would do anything for me. But I will leave it now to anyone who has had the same experience I have had. I was also sorry to bid farewell to old Camp Michigan, where we had passed a pleasant winter.

We took a boat for Fortress Monroe, where we arrived in time to see the Monitor which had defeated the Merrimac, which had done so much harm to our navy, and had been sent back to Norfolk, where she remained and never came out again. We stopped close to the Monitor, and we could see where the balls from the Merrimac had struck here turret in several places. The same day we landed at the Fort, and from there went to Hampton, where we stayed a few days, and then we took up our march for York-town.

We had no tents, but each man was provided with a little shelter tent made of canvas, about six feet long and three feet wide, with a piece of oilcloth to put under us. We would drive small stakes, four in number, in the ground, stretch the canvas on the stakes, and put the oilcloth under us to keep out the moisture, and that was the only protection from the weather we had.

WE NOW DREW UP IN FRONT OF YORK-TOWN.

We sat down before Yorktown for a long siege. Our brigade was encamped about a mile from the place, and in a veritable swamp. Our tents had not come up, so I put a fly over a bush and called it our headquarters. But after the wagons came up we put up our little dog tents, as we called them, and when we tried to sleep we would crawl in and shut the tent up to keep the enemy out, for we had an enemy ready to take our blood at the first opportunity. Yet they were all mussicians, and as soon as night came on they would try to lull us to sleep with their singing, though their notes were always of one tone, as they sang "Cousin, cousin, cousin." But I had no use for such cousins, as they were winged reptiles in the form of the largest mosquitoes I ever saw. My only means of denfese was my pipe, and I smoked until they were stupified, and then I got some sleep.

When we got to Yorktown, I had nothing to eat. The wagons were in the rear and could not get up on account of the bad roads, and they were unable to reach us until the third day. But hunger gnawed just the same.

Gen. Hintzelman had given strict orders that no animal should be killed or anything disturbed which belonged to the citizens. Such orders are all very well, but a hungry stomach knows no law, for a soldier especially, where it is generally considered there is no hell for a soldier, except what he has to endure in a rough campaign or on the battle field. I was suffering a little hell of my own, for I was a very hungry man. Finally I spied a nice fat shoat, a pig of about ten months old. Having my revolver with me, I shot it. I only wounded him, and I dared not fire again for fear of attracting attention, so I drew my saber and plunged it into his heart. This was the only time my saber was ever stained with blood. Some of the members of the band came up and commenced skinning the pig. when who should ride along but Gen. Hintzelman and staff. Salutations were given,

and they passed on. I gave some of the meat to Col.
Terry and some to Major Fairbanks. The rest we
roasted on the coals, as we had no other cooking uten-
sils. We had no salt, and so ate it without. Now
my hunger for a time was quieted, and night was coming on, and no camp equipage, I was puzzled as to
where we would sleep. I told the band each to shift
for himself. Meantime I had my eye on the only
house to be seen, except those in the enemy's lines,
and it had been deserted by the inhabitants who had
fled to the enemy for protection. When I came to go
to it I found the hospital department had appropriated
it for a hospital. This barred me from that. But
upon looking around I discovered a small hen house—
the chickens had long since departed—and though
this was not a nice place to stop, it was better than
no shelter at all from the cold sea breezes of early
spring. Not for one moment supposing man or animal would dispute my claims, I took informal possession. It was very dark by this time, and I had no
matches. I felt my way around to see what there
might be. I got hold of a barrel that seemed to be
nearly full of something. As I myself had not for some
time been full of anything, I was happy to find some-

thing near full. I felt over the barrel to see what it
was, and when I put my hand into it I found some
straw which had no doubt been a hen's nest, and lying
upon the straw was something soft and warm which I
took for a cat, and called "Pussy, pussy, pussy." I
had about made up my mind I had one friendly com-
panion anyway, when, oh! oh! I was notified of the
nature of my comnion, or companions, as it proved,
for I had molested a nest of young skunks. For-
tunately for me, they were young; but they did the
best they could in extending their hospitality and lent
me all the perfume I required for some time, and then
quickly deserted their home and yielded the whole
place to me. I walked outside to take the fresh air,
but the stench spread on every side and extended to
the hospital, disturbing the doctors so that they came
down to investigate, and insisted on shooting me for
a spy in disguise who had taken refuge in this out-
building and being exposed by my betters. But when
I explained matters, they laughed at my ridiculous
situation, and deodorized myself and premepted claim
the best possible, and I remained there over night.
Meantime I had got quite used to the situation and
sat down on the barrel for repose. I fell asleep, or

as near so as an exhausted man could under such a
trying situation. I finally awakened, to find that the
contents of the barrel, which was ashes and straw, had
sunk down with my weight, and I was wedged into
the barrel with my limbs nearly paralyzed and aching
at every joint. I struggled manfully to free myself,
and I tried to straighten the kinks out of my limbs,
but oh! how lame and sore I was. It was now daylight and I went to headquarters, where the fly was on
the bush, but oh! ye gods! the greeting I received as
I passed along was enough to drive a man to destrac-
tion. My uniform was anything but attractive—and
the odor! Tom Moore says:

> "You may break, you may shatter,
>   The vase if you will;
> But the scent of the roses
>   Will linger there still."

Well, the scent I had received the night before, still
lingered.

The private soldiers had their shelter tents and
blankets and, with a few boughs, could make themselves comfortable; but I, like the son of man, had no
place to lay my head, and I was certainly not wanted
in the camps, for as I passed through, the cry with

the smell, went up to heaven, "Put him out! Put him out! Shoot him! Call a detail and bury him. Send him to the Dry Tortugas." The Dry Tortugas was a place where military criminals were kept. I had no other satisfaction than to say to myself, "Damn you, enjoy a little of the misery I have for the past twelve hours." Well, I lived through this torrent for three days, until the wagons came up with the baggage and a change of clothes. The man who laughed at my situation the most was my best friend, Comrade Stack, whom I have spoken of before and stated that his wife was keeping house in Washington with my wife. I determined to get even with him, which I did in the following manner:

After we had got settled down in camp life, for the weeks the siege was going on, I received a paper from my wife. Mr. Stack was with me while I was reading, when I suddenly stopped and, as if studying over the matter, suddenly broke out, "What do you think of this?" and I apparently read from the paper:

"A FOOLISH AND TERRIBLE SCANDAL.

"Mrs. Stack and Mrs. J. D. Elderkin, wives of officers of the Fifth and Third Michigan Infantry, are making themselves notorious by going to the hospitals and carrying delicacies to the best looking young men, and declaring that they have come from above."

Mr. Stack took it to heart and, without looking for it himself, went directly to his tent and wrote his wife as follows:

"Mrs. Stack, I have heard of your scandalous conduct. Inclosed find three hundred dollars. It is the last you will ever get from me. We have just been paid off, and here I am in this d—n swamp, expecting any moment my head will be blown off, and you— and you—going around enjoying yourself and making a d—n fool of yourself. Take this and go to h—l; it is the last money you will ever get from me. So, good-bye, your once happy husband."

When Mrs. Stack read this letter she commenced to cry. My wife asked her what was the matter, and she showed my wife the letter. As soon as my wife saw the letter she cried out, "Oh, goodness me, dry your tears; this is all the work of Jim. He has been playing one of his practical jokes. I will get a letter from Jim to-morrow and he will tell me all about it."

I wrote to my wife the next day and told her what I had done. When she got the letter she showed it to Mrs. Stack and said, "Do you see? I told you it was all Jims' work, and would come out all right." Well, of course, everything is "well that ends well, and this matter ended well, and I was even with Mr. Stack and things went on smooth.

I had a friend by the name of William H. Allen, who was a member of Company F, Second Michigan Infantry, and a clerk for Gen. Richardson. Mr. Allen was always present when I had anything good to eat. He will acknowledge this himself, for he lives in Evart, Mich.

I got acquainted with Mr. Allen through a relative, Professor Lyman E. Stowe, who lives at 131 Catherine street. He married my niece, and myself and wife were boarding at C. F. Bessinger's, 178 Catherine street, Detroit. As Mr. Bessinger is my brother-in-law, and uncle to my niece, Mr. Stowe's wife, Mr. Stowe was a frequent visitor to Mr. Bessinger's while

the Second Regiment lay at Fort Wayne, before starting for the front.

Mr. Allen, with members and officers of Mr. Stowe's
company, called with Mr. Stowe, so I became acquainted with them in this way, and I never regretted
these acquaintances, for it ripened into close friendship. While we lay at Camp Michigan, Henry, or
"Hank," as we called him, was a very constant visitor,
and this was kept up ever after as long as I was in the
service, as well as after we got home. While in front
of Yorktown he would call every day and tell us all
the news. He would come to my tent and stay for
half an hour or so and talk and be sociable; then he
would leave. As I said before, he was a clerk for
Gen. Richardson. While we were in front of Yorktown, it was customary for me to go around in front
of the enemy's works and see all I could. When I
would go, Hank would let me take the General's
glass, a very large one, and with it I could see all over
the city. On the west of us was a large plain, and just
in front of that was a strip of woods, where we had
our large cannon in a fort we constructed, in order to
bombard the fort at Yorktown when occasion required.
On the left our enemy had erected some masked bat-

teries, and not far from where we were encamped.
One morning, Hank, Sergeant Bishop and I went out
in an old cornfield to look at the fort they had built
in the woods. The corn had been picked from off the
stalks and the stalks left standing. I got on a stump
to look, and brought my glass to bear so I could see
what they were doing. I could see the cannon; they
were covered with black oilcloth, and were only six
hundred yards from where we were standing. I said
to my comrades, "I can see some cannon, and the men
are working there in the intrenchment. After I had
looked all I cared to, Allen said, "Let me look, Jim."
I got down from the stump and handed him the glass.
I said to him, "Now when you see them going to those
cannon and take the canvas off, you get down." So
after Mr. Allen had been there a minute or so, Sergeant Bishop got on the stump, and I repeated the
warning I had given before. Bishop had not been on
the stump a minute before he was shot through the
bowels by a ten-pound shell. His entrails strung out
two or three yards. We tried to take him away, but
as sure as we would attempt to go for him they would
fire at us, so we didn't try any more; but two men,
more venturesome than we, succeeded in taking him

away. Two men, one from our light battery, took a
stretcher and, by crawling on their stomachs, succeeded in taking him off. In a few days after this I
got the glass and went alone to look at Yorktown,
and in order to get as close as I could it was necessary
for me to pass our pickets immediately on the road
leading to Yorktown. So I went down until I came
to our pickets, and I asked the officer in charge if he
would let me pass. I told him I was capable of taking
care of myself, and that I would like to see their forti-
fications. Then he told the guard to let me pass. I
was in the woods at this time, but going a little farther
I came to an opening, and I could see all over the
town. The road I was on was straight. The tele-
graph wires were off the poles and lying on the
ground. In a short time I came to a rise of
ground, on the top of which was a chimney with an
old-fashioned fireplace. The house had burned, but
the chimney remained standing. When I came up to
this I stopped and took my glass and was looking at
the forts, when I saw someone approaching me coming up the hill. I thought that was queer, as I knew
it was none of our men, as he was coming from the
opposite direction from where our men were stationed.

As he came a little nearer, I could see he had on a uniform—coat and cap. I was standing close to the chimney. As he came nearer I could see he had a rifle. I could just see the top of his head and the muzzle of his rifle. He came up very stealthily, bending forward, and when he thought he was close enough, he knelt down on his knee and brought his piece to his shoulder and took aim at me. I could look right into the muzzle of his gun, and when I saw his piece was steady I got behind the chimney, but kept my eye on him to see if he did not come farther. All the arms I had was my sword and a revolver. These were no good for that distance. I heard some sound on my right, or thought I did, and on keeping well under cover of my breastworks, I cast my eye in the direction from where I thought the sound came from, and who should I see but my deliverer in the form of one of Berdan's sharpshooters. He came up within fifty yards of my would-be murderer and shot him dead. I saw him fall. He was so intent on taking my life that he did not see the man who killed him. I don't know how the soldier who saved my life came to be where he was, unless he was sent out to keep his eye on me for fear something might happen to me. I never saw him before, or have I ever seen him since. I did not wait to thank him for what he had done, but went back to camp quicker than what I left it. The army was all ready to bombard Yorktown and was to commence the next day. But the next morning found Yorktown evacuated, and as we passed through in pursuit I closely observed the positions at the time I have been speaking of. The rebels had dug holes in the ground for picket posts. Of course the pickets of both sides were concealed by such methods.

We now followed in pursuit of the enemy towards Williamsburg. When near Williamsburg we could hear the firing. It was raining in torrents all day. The mud was very deep, so it was hard to make any progress, and, to make matters worse, Gen. Kearney would come riding back to hurry us up. He said he wanted the Michigan men to the front, so we went double-quick. When we got there we were formed in line of battle and the order was given to charge. The band and field music were ordered by Col. Terry to take position three paces in the rear of the colors. The rebels had felled trees in front of us, so we had to climb over them before we could see the enemy.

In our brigade were the Second, Third and Fifth Michigan and Thirty-seventh New York, an Irish regiment, and they were all brave soldiers. After the battle they gave us the name of the "Fighting Fifth," and we have kept the record ever since. The band and field music carried stretchers, and as a man would get shot we would put him on a litter and take him to the rear, where the doctors would attend him. The killed were left until after the battle; then a burial party would be detailed to bury the dead. Just after we went forward, two men were wounded, one a German, the other an Irishman. The German had two of his fingers shot off, and he complained bitterly. "Oh! mine Got! mine Got! I never can blay poker any more." The Irishman, who was more severely wounded, asked, "What the divil are you crying for? There's a mon there with his head off, and he don't say a dom word."

Our next battles were at Fair Oaks and the Seven Pines. These are matters of history, I shall not attempt to describe them.

After the Battle of Williamsburg we marched out to the White House Landing on the Pamunky River, thence back to Baltimore cross roads, where we encamped a few days preparatory to making a general advance. As soon as supplies were brought up we advanced, crossing the Chickahoming River, by the way of Bottoms bridge, to Fair Oaks and Seven Pines, where we fought these battles, and then fortified our position. We were now within eight miles of Richmond.

Our march to this point had been extremely difficult, on account of mud and general bad roads. The two battles were fiercely contested on both sides, and the loss for both sides very heavy. By this time the spring sun shown very hot and decomposition took place very rapidly, so that burial parties did their work under great difficulties, and many a dead soldier was barely covered with a little loose dirt, which the first rain would wash away. It was no uncommon thing to see a hand protruding from the ground, where a corpse had been buried in a cramped position, and the tention, as decomposition took place, caused the arm to spring out, not having much resistance from so little earth that had been placed over the body. Some facetious soldier, seeing a hand so protruding, would place a handful of cards therein as if the dead man was about to take a hand in a game of cards.

Our division and our brigade occupied the extreme left of the army, whose lines extended from White Oak Swamp to the right to Mechanicsville twenty miles away. This whole distance was fortified by breastworks, and daily picket duty was simply a continuous battle. The surgeons and the attendants were busy all of the time.

I had great difficulty to get some of the members of the band to perform the duty of surgeons' attendants, as they claimed, not being enlisted as a private soldier, they were only enlisted to make music, which in our case was really the fact. But there are some men always ready to perform any duty assigned to them, especially to relieve human suffering, while others would not take the risk of being shot to assist any one. I had some men who were never behind when help was called for. I will mention two in particular, one was Ollie Bloom, now in the postoffice; the other was Mr. Tagler, whom I before spoke of. These men, God bless them, never flinched duty.

Each day as the pickets were called on to go out on the line, I would be notified to send two men out to assist the surgeon to carry his instruments and stretchers and render such service as might be required.

I had a man by the name of Spiegel who played the baritone, and his twelve-year-old son beat the cymbals in our band. I ordered Mr. Spiegel to report for duty on the picket line, but he refused, as his papers said he need not do such service, and I was at a loss what to do with him when his twelve-year-old boy came up crying and said, "Mr. Elderkin, I wish you wouldn't send papa out, but let me go in his place." This was certainly a touching scene, and showed the nobility of the boy's nature. I told him neither of them needed to go, I would go myself. But from this incident forward I never had any trouble to get any of the men to go on duty when occasion required.

While we on the left were in a comparatively quiet but watchful state, heavy fighting was going on at the right. We did nothing but watch the enemy and pick huckleberries from the bushes and body lice from our clothing, for nature was prolific in her distribution of both. The huckleberries grew everywhere in profuse abundance, and such great big blue ones I never saw, and body lice seemed to breed in the very ground.

It was said no man, from the lowest private to the general in command, was able to keep entirely rid of them, and to aggravate matters more we neither had change of clothing or could we get water enough to drink, much less enough to wash in. A story once circulated that a private soldier was looking over his shirt for that kind of game when the general and staff passed by. The general spoke to the young man and asked, "What are you doing, picking off fleas?" The young man replied, "General, what do you take me for—a dog? No, sir, these are body lice."

One night I had an uncomfortable feeling come over me; it seemed to be shared in by our whole command. Something terrible must be about to happen. All day long the steady roar of artillery was going on at the right, and this seemed to grow more sullen and dense as night came on. The distant rumble, roll and thunder gradually drew nearer, and nearer, and nearer, until finally it died away as if all participants were wearied out and had sought a momentary rest. Sleep closed the eyes of all but the silent watches on the picket lines.

All too soon the gray of the morning dawn gradually stretched her silvery mantle over the face of the earth, quickly to be followed by the golden rays of a summer sun. But as quick as was this changing scene it was no quicker than the movements of the two mighty giants now up and preparing for the struggle of the day. Already the thunder of artillery could be heard away on the right, the whole army was in line, we were moved out of our camps, and no one need be told our right had been turned, and we must retreat or change our base of operation.

We had some new hospitals and quartermaster tents, and much army stores, which had to be abandoned; some of these I helped to destroy, so they would not fall into the enemy's hands, in good order.

Although we moved out of our camps early in the morning, we did not take up our line of march until afternoon. This was so as to allow the right wing to swing around and let our comparatively fresh troops cover the rear of the retreating forces. As our retreat lay still further to the left and rear of our position. Some of my regiment with a part of the Second Michigan Infantry had already crossed the White Oak

Swamp, and engaged the enemy who were trying to cut off our retreat from that direction.

Sunday night, June 29th, 1862, found the whole army across White Oak Swamp. Kerney's and Hooker's divisions had covered the retreat in a masterly manner.

Monday, June 30th, was clear and beautiful, and with the exception of here and there picket shots, little firing was heard until after ten o'clock in the morning. Then the troops were seen moving hurriedly in different directions, and we ourselves were marched rapidly into position, where we fought one of the most stubbornly contested battles of the war. This was called Charles City cross roads by the Northern forces and Frazier farm by the Southern forces. It was reported we were surrounded and must either cut our way out or be captured, and as is often the case when a little man is the under man in the fight the big fellow is getting the worst punishment. It was so in this case; though the enemy outnumbered us three to one, they received terrible punishment.

Kerney's and Hooker's divisions might possibly be sacrificed to give the rest of the army time to get in position and fortify at Melvern Hill. But such generals as Hooker and Kerney never give up while there is a ray of hope, and this fierce battle lasted well into the night, when both sides rested from sheer exhaustion. The early dawn saw our little army through the enemy's lines and well on our way to Melvern Hill. We passed through our lines at Melvern Hill early in the morning of Tuesday, July 1st. The enemy followed so closely that fighting began at once, and continued fiercely all day. Our position was admirably chosen, which gave our batteries great advantage and our gunboats on the James River played a prominent part. Five hundred pieces of artillery were thundering at one time. This is said to be the greatest artillery battle of the war, even Gettysburg was second to it.

So far as position of the field was concerned, the victory of the past seven days' fighting belonged to Lee and his confederate forces, but he might have well said with Perseus, "Another victory like this and I am undone."

The morning of July 2nd saw us on our way to Harrison's Landing and Lee in full retreat to Richmond, both sides whipped and worn out. It rained all day and we reached Harrison's Landing to find a swamp or fields of mud. The tired army lay down and rested in the mud as best they could with mud and water under them and torrents of rain pouring upon them.

We lay at this point until the 15th of August. Our rations were pretty good except the corn beef; it was very bad and of coarse grain, and the boys called it "Salt horse, or mule meat." Certainly it was anything but fit to eat. But it was boiled and served up. Bloom and Tagler, for mischief, would pile great quantities of it before Mr. Kern's tent before he got up, and he would have to remove it before he could get out.

One night the enemy came up on the opposite side of the river and fired a few cannon shot into our camp and also burned one of our barges loaded with hay. This illuminated the whole camp, but the enemy was quickly put to flight.

This was the last I saw of army life, as there was an order to muster out of service all regimental bands. I then went to Washington to see my wife. We left Washington a short time after and came back to Detroit, where I bought a home, No. 140 East Elizabeth street, and lived there until 1888, when my wife died, on the 18th of July, 1888. After I returned to Detroit I took my old position in the Detroit Light Guard again, and was armorer and leader of their band. I was with that company from July, 1857, until 1888. Since that time I have been a member of the veteran organization. They were all gentlemen, and some of the happiest days in my life were spent with the boys of that company. I was doing well and the officers and the men took quite an interest in me, and did all they could to make it pleasant for me.

For a few years they elected me drum major every year at their annual election, and I always turned out with them as such. After I became leader of the band I went with them. I had all the playing I could do. Sometimes I would have from thirty to forty men engaged a day. The Detroit Light Guard assisted me very much in procuring jobs. I was very much amused when the Detroit Light Guards went to Cleveland to visit the Cleveland Grays, in return to a compliment paid the Light Guards of Detroit. We had a man in the company who was a sergeant by the name of Cowen: he was a doctor and a Scotchman. He had a suit of kilts, a very nice one too. The day we got there it was quite windy, and he was a large man, and fine looking; every one admired his looks. The band was playing on the street, and so the doctor got on the balcony so he could see and hear better. Well, you can imagine what a crowd gathered to see him in his kilts, and it being very warm he had no nether garments under his skirt. There was quite a breeze at the time which gently lifted his skirts, and the doctor was a bare sight to behold. The crowd was cheering and laughing, but the doctor was oblivious to it all. I don't know how long he would have stayed if General Williams, at that time captain of the company, had not appeared and told him he had better get off the balcony, as the ladies did not like to see him in so cool a dress. He turned out with the company whenever they appeared on the street with his kilts. There are a few men left of the old Detroit Light Guards who will remember all I have said in relation to the company, T. Palmer, Millert, D. Pierce, J. Pitman, Mart, Smith, Oliver Goldsmith, Chas. Taylor, Alfred Russell and a few others.

As I said before, they had to pay for all they got; they got nothing from the State. They would give

high-toned parties at the Russell House, and charge
ten dollars a ticket, and by that means would realize
from six to eight hundred dollars in one night. After
my wife died in 1888 I did nothing for the company;
age was telling on me, and so I left as armorer and left
off music. While I was in the band I had lots of fun.
I was always full of the old nick, and I would play
my jokes off as often as I could. Sometimes while
we were on the street waiting for the procession to
form we would play a piece or two while they were
getting ready, and on such occasions there would be
a large crowd looking at us. I would take my cornet
and hit a man on the left of me on his shoulder, looking at the same time in the opposite direction. Of
course the man didn't know who hit him, so in a
minute I would repeat the dose. Some of the out-
siders would get on to it and would laugh; the man
who had been hit would say to the one who was laughing, you do that again and I will give you one in the
mouth; every one would laugh.

I have been walking on the street sometimes, and
a man would be in front of me, and I would take a
small piece of paper and do it up in a wad, and cough
and spit, at the same time I would throw it at the

man and hit him on the back. He would turn around and say, did you spit on me. I would say no. He would not take my word for it and take his coat off in the street.

We had a lot of crape in the armory that had been used on our collars, that had become dirty and useless; we had no more use for it, so I thought I would have some fun with it, so I took quite a piece and made a roll of it about the size of a small cat, and tied about fifty yards of strong black thread at one end of it, and started home at nine o'clock; I went to the corner of Randolph and Jefferson avenue, and let it fall on the sidewalk, and started to walk cross the street, and kept the end of the string in my hand, and took up the slack. I drew it on after me. When near the corner of Randolph and Jefferson a lady was crossing the street, and as she was crossing the crape went under her clothes and she jumped about three feet high and screamed. Every one ran to see what the matter was; they said, what is it? What is it; there it goes following that man. I commenced to haul in the slack. I did not want to get over my pleasure too soon. But I saw a man coming from his work, and he was running to catch up with the thing. There was quite a number following now. I was pulling in the slack, and it was only six feet from me, when the man who was so close put his foot on it, and his foot went down with such force it threw him down, and he looked up at me and smiled so foolish. He could feel nothing under his foot, and he did not know what to think of it. I took it home and my wife was resting on the lounge, and I told her what I had done, and commenced to laugh, and she laughed so hard she cried, and then said, "Jim, Jim, will you ever be a man; you have been a boy long enough; it is time for you to be a man." But I must believe my boyish tricks and ways preserved my youth, for I am still youthful feeling at seventy-eight, and I would advise my fellow-men to retain their youth by retaining their youthful ways.

OTHER AMUSING EXPERIENCES.

I have always been quite a story teller, and love to entertain my friends with anecdotes and story, and the following are some of my experiences and stories:

A DOG STORY.

I had a splendid dog, he was a spaniel, his name was Sport, I loved him as a brother, I supposed I loved him too much, but I could not help it. He was always so good, he would do most anything for me. When I would come home he would go to the closet and get my slippers for me, and then he would take my shoes. If I wanted a newspaper all I would have to do would be to say, "Sport, master wants a paper," and he would go and get me one. If I was on the street and dropped anything he would bring it to me. I took him with me wherever I went, and he was the only company I had since I lost my dear wife. When I was sad he would lay on the floor and watch me, and seemed to know I was feeling bad, and he would shed tears like a human being.

One night I was to play on an excursion for the Odd Fellows from Windsor. The band took the ferry at the foot of Woodward avenue and crossed the river. After we got over we went to the Crawford House and played two or three pieces, and after that went on board the boat we were to play on. After we got

on board the boat I missed poor Sport. I thought I
would never see him again. After the thing was over
the boat took us on the American side. It was about one
o'clock p. m. when we landed and I got on the dock
at Woodward avenue. What did I see but my poor
lost dog, who had taken the next ferry boat and came
home.

I am telling the truth and want to impress on the
minds of the reader the intelligence and love of a
dog. I could tell a great many more things he has
done, but my reader would not like to hear so much
about a dog. Just a few more words on the same
subject and I am through. In warm weather I would
take Sport on the boat and go to Belle Isle Park. This
was before the park was improved. Sport liked the
water, and I took much pleasure in seeing him enjoy
himself. I would take him on the boat to the island,
and when we landed he would run down the gang
plank and jump off the boat on the dock, and from
there in the water. One day I took him there, and the
boat was crowded, it being in the afternoon. As now,
in warm weather, vast numbers congregated there.
When Sport jumped on dock he looked at a notice
written on a blackboard that said no dogs allowed on
this island. As soon as he saw it he jumped off the

dock into the water. Some of the ladies called to me and said, "Mr. Elderkin, your dog has fallen in the river; he will be drowned." "No, I said, "he will swim ashore; he saw that notice," pointing to the notice on the blackboard, "no dogs allowed in the park." "Can he read?" they asked. Sport would swim to the shore before I could get there, and then I would go on the dock lower than the one you take in going off, and I would throw sticks and anything I could find in the water so he could bring it to me. I never took Sport any farther than the foot of the park, and after he had had a good time I would take the next boat home. This day I stayed longer than usual. A young man came to see Sport play in the water, and we had quite a chat together. As we were standing looking at the dog, I noticed a small boat moored at the low dock, and in a minute a young girl, fifteen or sixteen years old, went in the boat and left a basket of food, her parasol and a large sized book in the boat, and then came out, and seemed to be waiting for some one. In a few minutes her father came, jumped from the dock in the boat, and he nearly went through the boat. I said, "Now you will see some fun; that man don't know anything about a boat." In a few minutes more his wife came, and she came close to the boat, and the man got on the side of the boat to lift his wife down; she put her dress around her feet, and he put his arm up to receive her; it was about three feet down to the boat; as he got hold of her the boat tipped on one side, and filled with water. In their fright she fell overboard and he fell backward in the boat. The water was not deep. I ran and got hold of the line and pulled the boat in. The young man with me took hold of their hands and got them out. When the woman went down she was very much frightened, and both of them got a good soaking. When the lady came out I said, "You had a duck for supper." She made no reply. "Now," said the girl to her mother, "Go and see if you can get some dry clothes to put on."

As a matter of course we stayed to see the thing out. In a little while we saw a small boat approaching containing two young ladies, who came quite close to the place we were standing. They recognized the man with me and asked him if he would like to ride. He replied he would. They rowed the boat ashore and he got in. His weight of course caused the boat to settle on the ground. He took an ore

and shoved the craft off. As they commenced to
make some progress in the river he was telling the
girls about the accident. When the girl still standing
on the dock overheard him telling them of this, she
cried out, "It is a good thing the fools are not all
dead yet." Oh! how every person who heard the re-
mark laughed. It makes me smile every time I think
about it. She said nothing to me, but she looked
daggers at me. After I went home where I was room-
ing, then at 383 Brush street, corner of Montcalm, I
was reading the Free Press, and it came to my mind
and I had to laugh again. Where I had my room
there were some students who occupied rooms on the
same floor, and I woke sometimes in the night and I
had to laugh again, and I was afraid I would disturb
the students, but I didn't; so I had my fun all to myself and Sport. The next morning I asked the men
if they heard me laugh during the night, and they
said they did not. Then I told them of it, and they
all had a good laugh too.

I tell you, laugh all you can, it won't hurt you; you
will get fat if you can have a spell of it two or three
times an hour. The students said they didn't know
what they should do if it was not for me telling them

such funny stories. Whenever I came home they met me with smiles.

Here is a riddle, can you make it out? I will give one of my books to the first person who answers it. It runs this way:

Johnny looked down in the spring one day,
And what did he see but a dipper;
The handle crooked, the bottom out,
Yet floating about like a skipper.
It wasn't broken, good as new,
And fit for a monarch's daughter.
"Oh, you are a funny old dipper," said Johnny,
"You can't hold a drop of water."

A SLIGHT MISUNDERSTANDING.

The following story was another which amused the students very much:

At a mountain resort a young man by the name of Smith, not "John Smith," met a young lady by the name of Bell Hubbard; they were stopping at separate hotels. They were very fond of each other's society and every one could see it was a genuine love match. One night they were noticed to be in an unusually happy mood and the following conversation took place.

"My dear darling Bell, isn't this a beautiful summer night? The grand mountain scenery on every hand, and the cool mountain breeze to fan your heated brow. What a fitting place to form resolutions or make a binding contract. In fact, dear Bell, what a glorious place to pop the question, and here it goes. Will you take me for better or worse, will you take me for your husband, take my name and become Mrs. Smith?"

She replied, "Yes, Mr. Smith, I like your straight-forward and businesslike manner. I love frankness and honor."

Hugs and kisses were indulged in and they separated for the time. She was called aside by some lady friends, and he went out on the porch to take a smoke and talk over a fishing expedition of the next day, where speckled trout were to be found in plenty. Now Bell was somewhat speckled, too, as the sequel will show.

The next evening when Mr. Smith called on Miss Hubbard, he found things very much changed, instead of smiles and kisses he was met with a frown. Said he, "My dear Bell, what has come over you?

What is the matter? When I left you last evening you were so happy and all smiles. What has changed you so?" Said she, "Mr. Smith, I don't wish to speak to you. I hate you. I now know what kind of a man you are. I know, sir, I have got freckles, but I thought you were more of a gentleman than to make fun of me on that account." Mr. Smith was astonished and replied, "Why, Bell, I never did any such a thing." Said she, "Mr. Smith, you need not deny it to me. Last evening after we separated you went out on the porch and I overheard you say to Mr. Brown, 'Oh! Tom, what pleasure it is to come up to the mountains and catch these speckled beauties.'"

"Oh, my goodness, Bell," said Mr. Smith. I was talking about speckled trout and not beautiful girls that had a few freckles which only added to their beauty." Of course this set matters right.

A STINGY WOMAN.

I told my student friends that I boarded with a very close figuring landlady once, who carried a loaf of bread under her arm, and a knife in her hand, and asked each one if he would have another piece of bread, as she cut it when they wanted it, so as not to have any left over. This was all very well, but when she came to catch the flies who had been in the sugar bowl, merely to brush the sugar from their feet, that it might not be wasted, it was too much for my student friends and they charged me with exaggeration. I partially acknowledged the corn by saying I was no doubt like the very

WISE BOY,

who, seeing the stingy mother took good care of the whips she used on him, as she kept them over a motto, "God Bless Our Home," he said she ought to keep them over the other motto. She asked him why, and he said because it reads, "I need thee every hour." This seemed to please the boys immensely, but when I told them of

A WINKING FISH STORY

it broke them all up. This is a true story with a very little exaggeration.

But, by the way, I do not want the reader to judge all of my experiences which are truthful with these narratives of fun and exaggeration. But of course we are all in matters of fun a little like the deacon in church who was accused of exaggeration, and he replied that he had shed barrels of tears over that very sin.

It is a fact there is a wealthy gentleman in St. Johns, Michigan, by the name of George W. Emmons. I know this to be a fact because Mr. Emmons, for his first wife married my niece, and for his second wife married some one else's niece, and for his third wife he married my wife's niece.

Now Mr. Emmons is a mighty hunter and fisher, and as there is not more than a washtub full of water within many miles of St. Johns, Mr. Emmons must have an artificial lake in his backyard, stocked with whale, alligators, sturgeon, and all other varieties of the piscatorial tribe. This lake must be deep enough and large enough for a fifty-foot log to extend out into it; where his boys, Walter, Fred and Clarence, can dive from, when they go swimming; besides, it must be the log Mr. Emmons walks out on when he shoots fish. It must be so, for I heard him tell my wife that one morning he took his gun and went out to shoot a fish, and walking out on a log he spied a sturgeon or some other big fellow, and drew up his gun and fired at the fish. Somebody had rendered extra service and given his gun an extra charge, which caused the gun to express its indignation for being so overloaded, and it kicked him off of the log so he got a duck instead of a fish. He always declared the fish winked at him. But this was about the time he was looking for his third wife, and he was susceptible to winks at that time.

THE STORY OF A PARROT.

I was telling the students of a story of my experience. When I was in San Francisco, next door to my office was a restaurant. They kept a parrot, and one day I heard a terrible scolding going on; it seemed to be a woman's voice, which said as it increased in volume, "Don't you dare to strike me, don't you strike me, stand back, don't you touch me; then take him off, take him off, he will kill me," and then a terrible scream. I rushed in, but there was no one in the room but a parrot hanging in a large cage. It cried out, "Oh, what a fool you have made of yourself." This was the finest talking parrot I ever heard.

The story pleased everybody, and called forth the story of

THE PARROT AND THE MONKEY.

A parrot getting out of its cage was seized by a monkey, and its feathers stripped off. When the lady of the house came in and saw the plight of the bird and disordered room she threw up her hands and cried, "Oh, dear, what is the matter?" The parrot replied, "We have had a hell of a time."

Some one suggested this was an old story, and requested more of my war experiences. So I repeat one I forgot to mention in my Florida experience.

One day when in the Everglades in Florida my company, D, of the Fourth U. S. Infantry, were sent out in search of an expedition under the command of Major W. J. Graham. We were to look for a small detachment of marines under command of Captain McLochlen of the schooner Flirt, who were to come up a small stream of water in small boats. When we reached the creek it was very small; the parties we were looking for were not there; we remained there part of two days, and our rations being exhausted, we could not wait any longer, and we had to return without accomplishing our mission. We had no tents with us, nor were we permitted to make any fires in the night.

One night I became very thirsty after eating so much salt pork, and I did not take the precaution to fill my canteen before I laid down, and went to a little stream of water to fill my canteen. I took a drink, and after that I filled my canteen. I started to return to my comrades as I thought. I walked for some time, and I could not find the place I left a few moments before. I stopped and listened, but could hear no sound, and dare not make any noise, for fear the Indians would hear me, and I knew if any of the sentinels who were on guard would see me they would shoot me, for they had orders to shoot any one approaching from the outside. It was so dark I could hardly see my hand before me, and this in the thick woods. I did not know what to do. I could hear no sound of any kind. As I was standing bewildered, all at once what did I hear but "Who cooks for you" came from an owl right over my head. "I cook for myself," said I in my mind. I tell you it frightened me terribly, for I did not at first know but it was an Indian signal.

1 kept very quiet and I was compelled to stay in that place all night until daylight. And when it became light enough to see there I was within a few rods of my comrades, who wondered at my absence and laughed at my misfortune. But I tell you I was careful after that to get water before dark or take my bearings when leaving camp in an unknown locality.

My experience at the G. A. R. encampment at Buffalo. When we were ordered to take our position in line in the morning I thought I could stand the march, but after going ten or twelve blocks to the place designated I found I could not endure so long a march, and I was taken with cramps in my stomach, and I suffered a great deal. I went into a store and sat on a dry goods box, and while I was there Gov. Pingree came to see me, and he ordered an ambulance to take me to my quarters, 138 Delaware avenue. I had a fine room then on the first floor. I had the room all to myself, and would have had a good time had it not been for my sick spell. They put me in the ambulance and took me home. That is the first time I ever rode in such a conveyance. It hurts my feelings very much after my long service in the army to have to ride in a sick wagon. After I went home I got better in a little while, and some of my comrades said I ought to go and see the living shield only one block from where I was quartered and on the same street. It was the most beautiful sight I ever saw There was two or three thousand school children, most all of one size. They were placed on elevated benches from the ground up. The first row of seats was on the ground, the second tier a foot higher, and so on. They were all dressed to correspond with the colors of the shield, and formed the most magnificent spectacle I ever saw. As I was looking at it and seeing the Grand Army posts coming up on another street, two ladies approached me and said a few words to me, and then asked me if I would like to take a glass of wine. I told them I would. They were living only two or three doors from here. I went with them, and when we came to their house I was surprised to see such a magnificent house, everything was so very fine. They told me to take a chair on the porch, and one of them went in the house and in a few minutes returned with a decanter of whisky and one of wine, also with crackers and cheese, and told me to make myself happy. While I was doing justice to what was set before me one of the ladies asked me if I would like to take a ride around the city. If I would they would drive down to Camp Jewett, out some distance from where we were. They said the President and Gen. Alger would be at the camp. The camp was situated in a lovely locality, on the bank of the Niagara River, and a regiment of the regular U. S. Infantry, I think it was the Thirteenth Infantry, was located there. I thought no more about it and went to my room. I had not been there ten minutes when a splendid carriage drove up with two ladies in it, and stopped in front of the room I was in. One of them got out of the vehicle and ran up the steps, and I met her at the door. The carriage was the most magnificent one I ever saw. It had but one seat in it, and we sat pretty close together, one on my right and one on my left. So you see I was well taken care of. The driver had a silk hat on his head with a cockade on his hat, and metallic buttons on his coat. He drove as fine a pair of horses as I ever saw. We drove around the city for some time, and then we went down to camp; you ought to see the attraction we created. I never had the honor shown me as I did on this occasion; every person we met on the street would take off their hats. I had all of my medals on my breast, and the ladies were very richly dressed, and I looked like a general if I was not one, only surgeon of the Fairbanks Post No. 17, G. A. R., Department of Michigan. I think the old veterans took me to be Gen. Bombastes Furioso. We did not see the President; he had not got through with the procession, and so we had to go home without the pleasure of seeing his excellency. On our way home one of the ladies asked me if I would give her my photo. I told her I would with pleasure; that I would take one to her the next day. The next morning I took one over to her house, but she was not in. But when she came home she wrote me a letter with her monogram on the letter and also on the envelope, stating her regrets at being out when I called, and said she owned the carriage, and it was at my disposal whenever I felt disposed to avail myself of it. When I came to Detroit after the encampment I gave the letter to our adjutant comrade, Backus, to read at the post meeting the next Monday night, and the Post gave her a vote of thanks. They were very fine people and very wealthy. They were patriotic and they liked to do all they could for the G. A. R. It was unfortunate I was not well; I would have had a good time. The following is a copy of the letter sent me:

189 Delaware Ave., Buffalo.

Mr. J. D. Elderkin:

Dear Sir—I am sorry I was not home when you called this morning, but was happy to hear you was feeling better, and was delighted with the photograph; I shall prize it highly, and the G. A. R. will never be mentioned but it will recall to memory one friend I made at the encampment of '97. Hoping you may soon regain your health and enjoy many more meetings of your noble comrades, I remain,

Very sincerely,

ALICE F. HOLLIDAY.

August 26th.

THE ENCAMPMENT AT ST. PAUL.

When the G. A. R. went to St. Paul, Minn., we went on the F. & P. M. Railroad, and on our way to Ludington I bcame acquainted with a young lady and her mother, who were also going to the same place, who had friends there, and the young lady had availed herself of her vacation offered her of two weeks. She being a friend of the old soldiers, thought she would go and see the grand parade, and see if she could not do something to make it pleasant for the old boys, and it was not long before she had an opportunity to show her gratitude to us. When we arrived at Ludington, the boat that was to take us to Milwaukee was lying at the dock, and we went on board of her, thinking, however, we would all be provided for with berths, but when we went to the office for them we were told they were all engaged. You ought to have seen the picture of despair depicted upon the faces of the boys; standing room was at a premium. The steward told the ladies he could give each one of them a cot, but none for the men; they must do the best they could. We were told we would all have staterooms, but they did not keep their word. The rooms had all been engaged two days before. About eleven o'clock they commenced putting the cots in their places, and as one was ready someone would take possession of it.

I sat looking at those who were putting the cots in order, when the young lady I have spoken of before came to me and said, "Now, this cot is for me, you take it. I can sit up better than you can." I told her

I could think of nothing of the kind. It would not hurt me to sit up and it might make her sick to be deprived of her rest. It was no use for me to refuse; she said if I did not take it someone else would, for she would not take it herself. I saw there was no other way for me but to sleep on it. The cots were put close together, two on each side of the boat, leaving a passage in the center. When I got ready to go to bed I saw something on the cot next to the one I was to occupy—someone on it who had long hair. It startled me somewhat, for I had not laid so close to anyone wearing long hair since my wife died ten years ago. But I knew there was no danger of robbery, as the lights were going all night. I was very much disturbed in my sleep; the long hair semed to upset me somehow. After we got to Milwaukee we got on the cars and everything was all right. After we had been on the road some time I took a seat with the young lady and her mother, and sat with them quite a while, and then excused myself and went on the other side and talked to some of my friends. While I was there we passed through a tunnel. Wasn't I mad! I told the lady I was vexed, and she asked me what it was about, and I told her if I had known we

were going through a tunnel I would have stayed
with them. After I got to St. Paul I lost sight of her
and did not see her until I came to Detroit. She is a
very prety girl, and I never will forget her for her
kindness to me.

THE WASHINGTON ENCAMPMENT.

MY EXPERIENCE IN WASHINGTON DURING THE G. A| R. ENCAMPMENT.

After we arrived in Washington I thought I would
see if I could find a room, as I did not like the accommodations where we were stationed in a school-
house, so I went down to Seventh street, only two
blocks away. As I got on Seventh street I saw a
fine-looking house that had been recently painted,
with quite a number of flags displayed. Everything
looked so nice and clean that I thought I would like
to stay there. I went to the door and rang the bell.
A lady answered the summons, and I told her my mission. She said they had but one vacant room, and
that was on the second floor. If I would like to look
at it she would be pleased to show it to me. I went

into the house and she took me upstairs and I made an inspection of the room. Everything looked clean and nice. I asked the price, and she told me. I said I would take it for four days, and gave her the money in advance. It seems, her mother was the landlady, and did all the work, and her daughter got all the proceeds from the roomers. They had about eighteen or twenty who occupied rooms during the encampment. It was quite a lot of money they would take while we were there. The daughter had but recently been married, and worked in a small room in the back of the house, at dressmaking. I told her that I wanted the room to myself. After I came there at night I read the newspaper some, and after I had a good smoke from my pipe, turned down the gas and went to bed, thinking all the time I was alone. But after I had been in bed some time, I found I was not alone. I had hundreds of visitors, and I might say thousands. I was not very long in finding out the nature of my company. I got out of bed and turned on the gas and—Jerusalem! what a sight. The pillow slips and sheet were black with my enemy. I went right into battle. I think I must have slaughtered two or three hundred that night. I did not know what to do. I took a smoke, and after staying up for an hour or so I got so sleepy that I had to try it again. I slept quite well after the battle. In the morning I called the young lady to come in the room. I said to her, "Didn't you tell me I could have this room all to myself?" She said, "There was no one else with you, was there?" "I should think not," and told her to look at the pillows and sheets. I said to her, "Didn't you know the state of this room when I took it?" "No," she said. "Who slept here before I came?" said I. "My papa," said she. "Well," said I, "he must have a skin like an alligator." She said she would have the mother fix the room up. So I said nothing more and went away. But I knew what they would do, and when I returned I found the place exactly as I expected—the pillow slips turned inside out and the sheets turned over; that was all; so I went out and got a bottle of aqua ammonia and returned. When I turned down the cover to go to bed, I saw the enemy drawn up in line of battle, their eyes gleaming in the gaslight. But I made a flank movement and fired my ammonia by batallion and batteries and in brigade all down each side of the bed. This unexpected attack put the enemy to rout entirely and from this on for my brief stay I had the field to myself. But it was a desperate battle; I lost much blood in the first engagement, but none in the second.

AS MEMBER AND LEADER OF THE LIGHT GUARD BAND.

As a member and leader of the Light Guard Band I have met with many amusing and interesting events. .My associates were of course, for the time being, my business partners, and I cannot recall any unpleasant associations; but, on the contrary, there are many pleasant memories to linger over.

Our many attempts to please the public, by giving free concerts in the parks and public places, have been greeted with such enthusiastic outpouring of good-natured appreciation of our efforts that it leaves a wide roadway, strewn with flowers of sweet memory, to cheer me in my decling years, and brings back sweet memories in

RETROSPECTION.

In looking back I view my association with that grand military organization, the Detroit Light Guard, with much satisfaction and pride. Why should I not be proud to be an associate with such noble spirits as those who have composed the membership of that organization, many of whom have reached positions of high distinction?

To mention names of the more successful would be an injustice to the number who were equally worthy, though less fortunate. During my many years with them I have seen its membership changed by the coming and going, until I could appreciate the feelings of Eugene Sue's "Wandering Jew," who saw the rise of many generations and was left alone to view in retrospection the many faces which had passed before him.

It is not my purpose to enter into details of the organization or its many joyous annual reunions, for that is published in their historic records. But I wish to say that at each reunion that body of noble men have ever recognized my long service by rendering honorable mention of my name and other more substantial tokens of their kindness; and in my business of music they were ever associating me by reference and favoritism. I would never tire of singing the praises of this organization. But there has been so much published elsewhere, and by the press, and said so much better than I could say it, that I must leave the praise and records to much more worthy pens than mine.

I would also like to sing the praise of Fairbanks Post, G. A. R., God bless them!—every member They have ever stood ready to do me honor. But their record is too dazzling for my weak pen to even try to attempt, as it has been so much better written by others.

Of the press, I would speak and extend my thinks. The Detroit papers, especially the Free Press, have so often given me favorable mention, and sang my praise as an old veteran, that as my declining years bring me nearer and nearer to the shore I feel a joy mingled with sadness—the joy of receiving kindness from so many friends, and sorrow at the prospect of parting from them.

Last, though not least, I must speak of our beautiful city, where I have made my home so long, and seen it grow from a rambling old town to a mighty city; and in all of my many years' residence I have never had unpleasant altercations or trouble with any of its citizens. For the most part, my life has been serene; my pathway a pleasant one. I sincerely hope my friends who have read the book may take as much pleasure in reading it as I have in writing it and reviewing my past life.

J. D. ELDERKIN.

GRANT'S MANNER OF LIFE AT SACKET'S HARBOR AND DETROIT.

My acquaintance with Lieut. Grant was at Corpus Christi, at the beginning of the Mexican war. He was a very mild spoken man—spoke like a lady, almost. He always asked his men to do their duty; he never ordered them in an offensive way. He was about as nice a man as I ever saw. He was wonderfully cool and quick in battle. Nothing ever rattled him. He took an active part in every battle, and was quartermaster besides. I saw a great deal of him at Fort Vancouver, W. T., through the Mexican war, and then at Detroit and Sacket's Harbor, after the war. He was very sociable, always talked to a man freely and without putting on the airs of a superior officer. I remember him very well at Detroit. I also remember his wife very well; I used to carry the mail, sometimes twice a day, to their house on Fort street east. He used to ride and drive a great deal; at Sacket's Harbor I remember he used to practice with clubs. He lived very modestly—he couldn't afford to do anything else on his pay. His only dissipation was in owning a fast horse; he always liked to have a fine horse, and he paid well for them. While Grant did not dance, he played cards occasionally, and checkers also. He read whatever he could find to read, and read aloud to his wife; and in this quiet way was a tender, though undemonstrative, husband and a good citizen.

I wish to say in regard to my acquaintance with General Grant, not that I could add one iota to the luster of the record of the grand old General, but for the satisfaction that it gives me to relate of my close personal acquaintanceship with such a noble man, and my service in the field and camp with him and my knowledge of him in civil life, I always found him the same quiet, unassuming, noble man.

J. D. E.

www.ingramcontent.com/pod-product-compliance
Lightning Source LLC
Chambersburg PA
CBHW030825270326
41928CB00007B/892